P.K. Withrow

ETHICS

PRENTICE-HALL FOUNDATIONS OF PHILOSOPHY SERIES

Virgil Aldrich	Philosophy of Art
William Alston	Philosophy of Language
Stephen Barker	Philosophy of Mathematics
Roderick Chisholm	Theory of Knowledge
William Dray	Philosophy of History
Joel Feinberg	Social Philosophy
William Frankena	Ethics
Carl Hempel	Philosophy of Natural Science
John Hick	Philosophy of Religion
David Hull	Philosophy of Biological Science
Willard Van Orman Quine	Philosophy of Logic
Richard Rudner	Philosophy of Social Science
Wesley Salmon	Logic
Jerome Shaffer	Philosophy of Mind
Richard Taylor	Metaphysics

Elizabeth and Monroe Beardsley, editors

second edition

ETHICS

William K. Frankena

UNIVERSITY OF MICHIGAN

PRENTICE-HALL, INC.

Englewood Cliffs, New Jersey

Library of Congress Cataloging in Publication Data

Frankena, William K
Ethics.

(Prentice-Hall foundations of philosophy series)
Bibliography p.
1. Ethics.
BJ1012.F7 1973 170 72–11836
ISBN 0–13–290478–0

Printed in the United States of America.

10 9 8 7 6 5 4 3

PRENTICE-HALL INTERNATIONAL, INC., London
PRENTICE-HALL OF AUSTRALIA, PTY. LTD., Sydney
PRENTICE-HALL OF CANADA, LTD., Toronto
PRENTICE-HALL OF INDIA PRIVATE LIMITED, New Delhi
PRENTICE-HALL OF JAPAN, INC., Tokyo

To Sadie

FOUNDATIONS OF PHILOSOPHY

Many of the problems of philosophy are of such broad relevance to human concerns, and so complex in their ramifications, that they are, in one form or another, perennially present. Though in the course of time they yield in part to philosophical inquiry, they may need to be rethought by each age in the light of its broader scientific knowledge and deepened ethical and religious experience. Better solutions are found by more refined and rigorous methods. Thus, one who approaches the study of philosophy in the hope of understanding the best of what it affords will look for both fundamental issues and contemporary achievements.

Written by a group of distinguished philosophers, the Foundations of Philosophy Series aims to exhibit some of the main problems in the various fields of philosophy as they stand at the present stage of philosophical history.

While certain fields are likely to be represented in most introductory courses in philosophy, college classes differ widely in emphasis, in method of instruction, and in rate of progress. Every instructor needs freedom to change his course as his own philosophical interests, the size and makeup of his classes, and the needs of his students vary from year to year. The nineteen volumes in the Foundations of Philosophy Series—each complete in itself, but complementing the others—offer a new flexibility to the instructor, who can create his own textbook by combining several volumes as he wishes, and can choose different combinations at different times. Those volumes that are not used in an introductory course will be found valuable, along with other texts or collections of readings, for the more specialized upper-level courses.

Elizabeth Beardsley / Monroe Beardsley

CONTENTS

3

UTILITARIANISM, JUSTICE, AND LOVE, 34

all

4

MORAL VALUE AND RESPONSIBILITY, 61

5

INTRINSIC VALUE AND THE GOOD LIFE, 79

6

MEANING AND JUSTIFICATION, 95

PREFACE

This book is intended to introduce students and general readers to the branch of philosophy called "ethics." I shall try, among other things, to present some of the standard material of ethics that beginners and others should know. This will not, however, be a summary of what moral philosophers are agreed upon, as introductions to other subjects may be summaries of what the experts in those fields agree upon. Such a substantial body of agreement does not exist in philosophy. Nor will this be simply an introductory review of the various differing positions moral philosophers have taken, although many of these positions will be presented and discussed. My aim in this book is not just to introduce the problems and positions of moral philosophers, but also to do moral philosophy. That is, I shall try to write an essay in moral philosophy in which I put forward some of my own views and reasoning, and at the same time, provide an introduction to the subject in general.

I try to do this because the proper purpose of an introduction like this must be, not merely to pass on information, but to stimulate and help the reader to do better, clearer, and more philosophical thinking about ethical questions than he would do otherwise. Such an introduction will involve my presenting answers or partial answers to some of these questions; however, these are not meant dogmatically and should not be taken as final unless they stand up under the reader's own scrutiny. I do not think that the only way for others to think better or more clearly is by their coming to agree with me. Their coming to disagree clearly and on carefully reasoned grounds will serve the purpose of this book as well. It is an introduction to the kind of thinking that *is* moral philosophy as I understand it.

In the spirit just indicated, let me say something about my arguments in this book. When I give arguments for or against a certain ethical position,

I am not thinking of them as conclusive proofs or disproofs. Such conclusive proofs or disproofs are as difficult as they are rare in philosophy. More about the nature of ethical judgments and their justification will come out as we go along, especially in Chapter 6, but I recognize that it is always logically possible for my opponent to stand pat in his position in spite of my arguments. My arguments are meant as arguments for or against positions all right, as they should be in philosophy, but not as irresistible forces or immovable objects. Rather they are statements of my reasons for taking or rejecting a certain view and invitations to the reader to consider whether they convince him that he should do likewise. My point is not to push him around; it is to bring him to see what position seems most reasonable to him, when, with such help as I can give him, he thinks things over. He always can hold out against me; the question then is whether he thinks his position is the most sensible one to take—not whether he *can* take it but whether he is willing to take it. The method is that of Socrates.

There are also times when I do not actually give arguments for what I say. This does not mean that I am simply being dogmatic. Partly, the reason is that there is not space to debate everything, but, mainly, it is that I am asking the reader to think about the matter in hand and to see if what I say does not seem on the whole the most reasonable thing to say and to hold. Once more, however, what matters is not whether he agrees or disagrees but whether he comes out with a more adequate ethical theory.

In this revised edition I have made many corrections, some stylistic or verbal, some expository, some doctrinal and substantive. There are also many additions of various sizes and sorts. The chief changes are: (a) a discussion of the divine command theory of right and wrong in Chapter 2, (b) a more elaborate review of utilitarianism in Chapter 3, (c) a further presentation of my own theory of obligation in Chapter 3, (d) more on the ethics of virtue in Chapter 4, (e) additional material on the good life in Chapter 5, (f) more on the distinction between moral and nonmoral judgments and on the moral point of view in Chapter 6, and (g) a revised and expanded bibliography.

I may also mention that *Introductory Readings in Ethics,* edited by W. K. Frankena and J. T. Granrose and closely correlated with my book, will be published by Prentice-Hall, Inc. shortly. I am indebted to my friends, students, family, and to other writers, for their assistance, which I gratefully acknowledge here.

William K. Frankena

CHAPTER ONE

Morality and Moral Philosophy

Suppose that all your life you have been trying to be a good person, doing your duty as you see it and seeking to do what is for the good of your fellowmen. Suppose, also, that many of your fellowmen dislike you and what you are doing and even regard you as a danger to society, although they cannot really show this to be true. Suppose, further, that you are indicted, tried, and condemned to death by a jury of your peers, all in a manner which you correctly consider to be quite unjust. Suppose, finally, that while you are in prison awaiting execution, your friends arrange an opportunity for you to escape and go into exile with your family. They argue that they can afford the necessary bribes and will not be endangered by your escaping; that if you escape, you will enjoy a longer life; that your wife and children will be better off; that your friends will still be able to see you; and that people generally will think that you should escape. Should you take the opportunity?

AN EXAMPLE OF ETHICAL THINKING (SOCRATES)

This is the situation Socrates, the patron saint of moral philosophy, is in at the opening of Plato's dialogue, the *Crito*. The dialogue gives us his answer to our question and a full account of his reasoning in arriving at it. It will, therefore, make a good beginning for our study. Socrates first lays down some points about the approach to be taken. To begin with, we must not let our decision be determined by our emotions, but must examine the question and follow the best reasoning. We must try to get our facts straight and to keep our minds clear. Questions like this can and should be settled by reason. Secondly, we cannot answer such questions by appealing to what people generally think. They may be wrong. We must try to find an answer we ourselves can regard as correct. We must think for ourselves. Finally, we ought never to do what is morally wrong. The only question we need to answer is whether what is proposed is right or wrong, not what will happen to us, what people will think of us, or how we feel about what has happened.

Having said this, Socrates goes on to give, in effect, a threefold argument to show that he ought not to break the laws by escaping. First: we ought never to harm anyone. Socrates' escaping would harm the state, since it would violate and show disregard for the state's laws. Second: if one remains living in a state when one could leave it, one tacitly agrees to obey its laws; hence, if Socrates were to escape he would be breaking an agreement, which is something one should not do. Third: one's society or state is virtually one's parent and teacher, and one ought to obey one's parents and teachers.

In each of these arguments Socrates appeals to a general moral rule or principle which, upon reflection, he and his friend Crito accept as valid: (1) that we ought never to harm anyone, (2) that we ought to keep our promises, and (3) that we ought to obey or respect our parents and teachers. In each case he also uses another premise which involves a statement of fact and applies the rule or principle to the case in hand: (1a) if I escape I will do harm to society, (2a) if I escape I will be breaking a promise, and (3a) if I escape I will be disobeying my parent and teacher. Then he draws a conclusion about what he should do in his particular situation. This is a typical pattern of reasoning in moral matters and is nicely illustrated here.

In this pattern of moral reasoning one determines what one should do in a particular situation by reference to certain general principles or rules, which one takes as premises from which to deduce a particular conclusion by a kind of practical syllogism, as Aristotle called it. One takes general principles and applies them to individual situations. How natural this procedure is will be apparent to any reader of the *Crito*. In all fairness, however, we must observe at this point that some moral thinkers have a different view of the logic of moral deliberation. As we shall see in Chapter 2 the act-deontologists and other proponents of "situation ethics" take particular judgments to be basic in morality, rather than general ones, which they regard as inductive generalizations from particular cases, if they recognize the existence of general rules at all.

It happens that in the *Crito* Socrates thinks his three principles all lead to the same conclusion. But sometimes when two or more rules apply to the same case, this is not true. In fact, most moral problems arise in situations where there is a "conflict of duties," that is, where one moral principle pulls one way and another pulls the other way. Socrates is represented in Plato's *Apology* as saying that if the state spares his life on condition that he no longer teach as he has been doing, he will not obey, because (4) he has been assigned the duty of teaching by the god, Apollo, and (5) his teaching is necessary for the true good of the state. He would then be involved in a conflict of duties. His duty to obey the state applies, but so do two other duties, (4) and (5), and these he judges to take precedence over his duty to obey the commands of the state. Here, then, he resolves the problem, not just by appealing to rules, for this is not enough, but by determining which rules take precedence over which others. This is another typical pattern of reasoning in ethics.

To return to the *Crito,* Socrates completes his reasoning by answering his friends' arguments in favor of escaping by contending that he will not really be doing himself, his friends, or even his family any good by becoming an outlaw or going into exile, and that death is not an evil to an old man who has done his best, whether there is a hereafter or not. In other words, he maintains that there are no good moral grounds on the other side and no good prudential ones—which would count only if moral considerations were not decisive—either.

All this is interesting, not just because it represents one of the classic discussions of the question of civil disobedience, but because it illustrates two kinds of moral problems and how one reflective and serious moral agent went about solving them. It also shows us much of Socrates' working ethics: principles (1) to (5) plus the second-order principle that (4) and (5) take precedence over the duty to obey the state. This duty to obey the state, by the way, is for him a *derivative* rule which rests on (1), (2), and (3), which are more *basic.* One can find out one's own working ethics by seeing how one would answer these two problems oneself, or others like them. This is a good exercise. Suppose that in doing this you disagree with Socrates' answer to the *Crito* problem. You might then challenge his principles, which Crito did not do. You might ask Socrates to justify his regarding (1), (2), and (3) as valid, and Socrates would have to try to answer you, since he believes in reason and argument in ethics, and wants knowledge, not just true opinion.

At this point Socrates might argue that (2), for example, is valid because it follows from a still more basic principle, say, (4) or (5). That is, he might maintain that we should keep promises because it is commanded by the gods or because it is necessary for the general welfare. But, of course, you might question his more basic principle, if you have any good reason for doing so (if you question without reason, you are not really entering into the dialogue). At some point you or he will almost inevitably raise the question of how ethical judgments and principles, especially the most *basic* ones, are to be justified anyway; and this is likely to lead to the further question of what is meant by saying that something is right, good, virtuous, just, and the like, a question which Socrates in fact often raises in other dialogues. (In the *Euthyphro* for example, he argues, in effect, that "right" does not mean "commanded by the gods.")

THE NATURE OF ETHICS OR MORAL PHILOSOPHY

When this happens the discussion has developed into a full-fledged philosophical one. Ethics is a branch of philosophy; it is *moral philosophy* or philosophical thinking about morality, moral problems, and moral judgments. What this involves is illustrated by the sort of thinking Socrates was doing in the *Crito* and *Apology,* supplemented as we have supposed it to be. Such philosophical thinking will now be described more fully.

Moral philosophy arises when, like Socrates, we pass beyond the stage in which we are directed by traditional rules and even beyond the stage in which these rules are so internalized that we can be said to be inner-directed, to the stage in which we think for ourselves in critical and general terms (as the Greeks were beginning to do in Socrates' day) and achieve a kind of autonomy as moral agents. We may, however, distinguish three kinds of thinking that relate to morality in one way or another.

1. There is descriptive empirical inquiry, historical or scientific, such as is done by anthropologists, historians, psychologists and sociologists. Here, the goal is to describe or explain the phenomena of morality or to work out a theory of human nature which bears on ethical questions.

2. There is normative thinking of the sort that Socrates was doing in the *Crito* or that anyone does who asks what is right, good, or obligatory. This may take the form of asserting a normative judgment like

"I ought not to try to escape from prison,"

"Knowledge is good," or

"It is always wrong to harm someone,"

and giving or being ready to give reasons for this judgment. Or it may take the form of debating with oneself or with someone else about what is good or right in a particular case or as a general principle, and then forming some such normative judgment as a conclusion.

3. There is also "analytical," "critical," or "meta-ethical" thinking. This

is the sort of thinking we imagined that Socrates would have come to if he had been challenged to the limit in the justification of his normative judgments. He did, in fact, arrive at this sort of thinking in other dialogues. It does not consist of empirical or historical inquiries and theories, nor does it involve making or defending any normative or value judgments. It does not try to answer either particular or general questions about what is good, right, or obligatory. It asks and tries to answer logical, epistemological, or semantical questions like the following: What is the meaning or use of the expressions "(morally) right" or "good"? How can ethical and value judgments be established or justified? Can they be justified at all? What is the nature of morality? What is the distinction between the moral and the nonmoral? What is the meaning of "free" or "responsible"?

Many recent moral philosophers limit ethics or moral philosophy to thinking of the third kind, excluding from it all questions of psychology and empirical science and also all normative questions about what is good or right. In this book, however, we shall take the more traditional view of our subject. We shall take ethics to include meta-ethics as just described, but as also including normative ethics or thinking of the second kind, though only when this deals with general questions about what is good or right and not when it tries to solve particular problems as Socrates was mainly doing in the *Crito*. In fact, we shall take ethics to be primarily concerned with providing the general outlines of a normative theory to help us in answering problems about what is right or ought to be done, and as being interested in meta-ethical questions mainly because it seems necessary to answer such questions before one can be entirely satisfied with one's normative theory (although ethics is also interested in meta-ethical questions for their own sakes). However, since certain psychological and anthropological theories are considered to have a bearing on the answers to normative and meta-ethical questions, as we shall see in discussing egoism, hedonism, and relativism, we shall also include some descriptive or empirical thinking of the first kind.

THE NATURE OF MORALITY

We have described ethics as philosophy that is concerned with *morality* and its problems and judgments, or with *moral* problems and judgments. It must be noticed, however, that the word "ethics" is not always used for this branch of philosophy; sometimes it is used as just another word for "morality," and sometimes to refer to the moral code or normative theory of an individual or group, as when I spoke earlier of "Socrates' working ethics." More important for our present purposes are some other facts about our usage of words. The terms "moral" and "ethical" are often used as equivalent to "right" or "good" and as opposed to "immoral" and "unethical." But we also speak of moral problems, moral judgments, moral codes, moral arguments, moral experiences, the moral consciousness, or the moral point of view. "Ethical" is used in this way too. Here "ethical" and "moral" do not mean "morally right" or "morally good." They mean "pertaining to morality" and are opposed to the "*non*moral" or "*non*ethical," not to the "*im*moral" or "*un*ethical." Similarly, the term "morality" is sometimes used as opposed to "immorality," as when we say that the essence of morality is love or speak of the morality of an action. But we also use the word "morality" to refer to something that is coordinate with but different from art, science, law, convention, or religion, though it may be related to them. This is the way we use the term when we ask, "What is morality? How does it differ from law? How is it related to religion?" In this sense "morality" means what Bishop Butler called "the moral institution of life." This is how I have been using "morality" and propose to go on using it. Correspondingly, I shall use "moral" and "ethical" in this sense also.

Now, morality in the sense indicated is, in one aspect at least, a social enterprise, not just a discovery or invention of the individual for his own guidance. Like one's language, state, or church, it exists before the individual, who is inducted into it and becomes more or less of a participant in it, and it goes on existing after him. Moreover, it is not social merely in the sense of being a system governing the relations of one individual to others; such a system might still be entirely the individual's own construction, as some parts of one's code of action with respect to others almost inevitably are, for example, "My rule is to smile first." Morality, of course, is social in this sense to a considerable extent; however, it is also largely social in its origins, sanctions, and functions. As first encountered by the individual, at any rate, it is an instrument of society as a whole for the guidance of individuals and smaller groups. It makes demands on individuals that are, initially at least, external to them. Even if the individuals become spokesmen of these demands, as they usually do to some extent through what is called "internalization," the demands are still not merely theirs nor directed only at themselves. If they come to disagree with the demands, then, as Socrates thought and as we shall see later, they must still do so from the moral point of view that has somehow been inculcated into them. One may think of society, as many people do, as having a supernatural dimension and as including a divine lawgiver, but even then one is ascribing this social character to morality.

Because of such facts, morality is sometimes *defined* as an instrument of society as a whole, as if an individual, family, or social class cannot have a morality or moral action-guide of its own that is different from that of its society. However, in view of what we shall be saying in a moment, it seems desirable to allow that smaller groups and even individuals may have or work out such distinct guides for their conduct, and to call at least some of these "value-systems" moralities or moral codes, namely, those that embody what we shall refer to as the moral point of view. Even so, it seems plausible to insist that an individual who has such a personal morality must be thinking that others besides himself, indeed his entire society, should adopt it or at least its more basic principles or ideals.

In any case, whether it is thought of as an instrument of society or as a personal code, morality must be contrasted with prudence. It may be that prudence and morality dictate some of the same conduct, for example, honesty. It may also be that prudence is a moral virtue; however, it is not characteristic of the moral point of view to determine what is right or virtuous wholly in terms of what the individual desires or of what is to his interest. In Freudian terms, morality and prudence are both attempts to regulate the id; but while prudence is simply a function of the reality-principle in the ego, morality is the function of a superego which does not think merely in terms of getting what is desired by the individual id or even in terms of salvaging the greatest balance of satisfaction over frustration for it.

Considered as a social system of regulation, morality is like law on the one hand and convention or etiquette on the other. All of these systems are social in a way in which prudence is not, and some of the same expressions are used in all of them, for example, the words "right" and "should." But convention does not deal with matters of such crucial social importance as those dealt with by law and morality; it seems to rest largely on considerations of appearance, taste, and convenience. Thus, morality is distinguished from convention by certain features that it shares with law; similarly, it is also distinguished from law (with which it overlaps, for example, in forbidding murder) by certain features that it shares with convention, namely, in not being created or changeable by anything like a deliberate legislative, executive, or judicial act, and in having as its sanctions, not physical force or the threat of it but, at most, praise and blame and other such mainly verbal signs of favor and disfavor. Some writers have even held that the only proper motives or sanctions for morality are purely internal ones like the sentiment of benevolence or the desire to do what is right for its own sake; there is much to be said for this view even if it hardly describes the whole practical working of morality. At least it highlights the fact that physical force and certain kinds of prudential considerations do not strictly belong to the idea of a moral institution of life.

However, morality, at least as it has developed in the western world, also has a more individualistic or protestant aspect. As Socrates implied and recent philosophers have stressed (perhaps too much), morality fosters or even calls for the use of reason and for a kind of autonomy on the part of the individual, asking him, when mature and normal, to make his own decisions, though possibly with someone's advice, and even stimulating him to think out the principles or goals in the light of which he is to make his decisions. Even as a social institution of life, morality is thought of as aiming at rational self-guidance or self-determination in its members. In Matthew Arnold's words, it asks us to be ". . . self-govern'd, at the feet of Law."

Accordingly, it has been usual for moral philosophers to distinguish stages of morality, which can be more or less clearly traced both in the history of our culture and in the life of the individual, to distinguish, for instance (a) "pre-rational," "customary," or "group" morality and (b) "personal," "rational," or "reflective" morality. Improving on this in an interesting and instructive way, David Riesman, a social scientist, has recently portrayed four moral or social types in *The Lonely Crowd:*

1. The tradition-directed individual and/or society.
2. The inner-directed individual and/or society.
3. The other-directed individual and/or society.
4. The autonomous individual and/or society.

The general idea here, and in much recent social psychology and moral philosophy, is that morality starts as a set of culturally defined goals and of rules governing achievement of the goals, which are more or less external to the individual and imposed on him or inculcated as habits. These goals and rules may and generally do, at least to some extent, become "internalized" or "interiorized," that is, the individual takes them as his own and regulates his own conduct by them; he develops a "conscience" or "superego." This process of internalization may be quite irrational but, as we shall see, it is typical for morality to accompany its inculcations with at least a modicum of reason-giving. Thus, we (and even the Navaho) tend to give reasons with our moral instructions as soon as the child has attained an age at which he is capable of something like discretion, and we even lead him to feel that it is appropriate to ask for reasons. That is why it seemed appropriate to Socrates, at his juncture in the history of Greece, to ask for definitions and arguments in matters of morals.

We may then, without leaving the moral fold, move from a rather irrational kind of inner direction to a more rational one in which we achieve an examined life and a kind of autonomy, become moral agents on our own, and even reach a point when we can criticize the rules and values of our society, as Socrates did in the *Apology* and the *Crito.* Some find too much anxiety in this transition and try to "escape from freedom" in one way or another (including other-direction), some apparently can make the transition only with the help of psychoanalysis, but for others it involves no major difficulties other than the use of some hard thought such as Socrates engaged in.

Clearly, it is in the last stages of this process that moral philosophy plays its natural role. We are then—or from now on may imagine ourselves to be—in the middle or later stages of the moral life as these were just outlined. It is the thinking to be done here that we mainly wish to help on its way, although we also hope, in spite of the element of danger involved, to pull those who are not so far along out of their unreflective nest and its dogmatic slumber.

FACTORS IN MORALITY

The institution of morality contains a number of factors: (1) certain *forms of judgment* in which *particular* objects are said to have or not to have a certain moral quality, obligation, or responsibility; (2) the implication that it is appropriate and possible to give *reasons* for these judgments; (3) some *rules, principles, ideals,* and *virtues* that can be expressed in more *general judgments* and that form the background against which particular judgments are made and reasons given for them; (4) certain characteristic natural or acquired *ways of feeling* that accompany these judgments, rules, and ideals, and help to move us to act in accordance with them; (5) certain *sanctions* or additional sources of motivation that are also often expressed in verbal judgments, namely, holding responsible, praising, and blaming; (6) a *point of view* that is taken in all this judging, reasoning, and feeling, and is somehow different from those taken in prudence, art, and the like. For our purposes, we may center most of our discussion on the moral judgments involved in factors (1), (3), and (5). These have a central place in morality, and the main questions of normative ethics and meta-ethics relate to them.

KINDS OF NORMATIVE JUDGMENT

Moral or ethical judgments are of various kinds. As has been indicated, they may be particular or general. They may also be stated in different persons and tenses. These differences are all important in their places, but here we must stress another difference. In some of our moral judgments, we say that a certain action or kind of action is morally right, wrong, obligatory, a duty, or ought or ought not to be done. In others we talk, not about actions or kinds of action, but about persons, motives, intentions, traits of character, and the like, and we say of them that they are morally good, bad, virtuous, vicious, responsible, blameworthy, saintly, despicable, and so on. In these two kinds of judgment, the things talked about are different and what is said about them is different. (We do also speak of "good actions" or "deeds," but here "good" is not properly used as a synonym of "right," as it often is; properly used, it seems to mean either that the action has a good motive or that it has good consequences.) I shall call the former *judgments of moral obligation* or *deontic* judgments and the latter *judgments of moral value* or *aretaic* judgments.

There are also *judgments of nonmoral value*. In these we evaluate not so much actions, persons, motives, and the like, but all sorts of other things: cars, paintings, experiences, forms of government, and whatnot. We say they are good, bad, desirable, undesirable, and so on, but we do not mean that they are morally good or morally bad, since they are generally not the kinds of things that can be morally good or bad. A study of these judgments is not, as such, a part of ethics or moral philosophy, though it is part of the theory of value in general. But since it will turn out that a consideration of what is good (nonmorally) is involved in determining what is morally right or wrong, we must include a discussion of such value judgments anyway.

For the sake of completeness, we must also recognize another kind of normative judgment, which I shall call *nonmoral judgments of obligation.* Examples appear in the following outline, but, as these examples will make clear, judgments of this kind have no special interest for *moral* philosophy and so do not call for discussion in a book on ethics, even though they are of considerable practical importance.

We obtain, then, the following outline of kinds of *normative judgment:*

I. Ethical or moral judgments proper:
   A. Judgments of moral obligation (deontic judgments):
      1. Particular, e.g. (assuming terms are used in their moral senses),
         a. I ought not to escape from prison now.
         b. You should become a missionary.
         c. What he did was wrong.
      2. General, e.g.,
         a. We ought to keep our agreements.
         b. Love is the fulfillment of the moral law.
         c. All men have a right to freedom.
   B. Judgments of moral value (aretaic judgments):
      1. Particular, e.g.,
         a. My grandfather was a good man.
         b. Xavier was a saint.
         c. He is responsible for what he did.
         d. You deserve to be punished.
         e. Her character is admirable.
         f. His motive was good.
      2. General, e.g.,
         a. Benevolence is a virtue.
         b. Jealousy is an ignoble motive.
         c. The man who can forgive such carelessness is a saint.
         d. The good man does not cheat or steal.
II. Nonmoral normative judgments:
   A. Judgments of nonmoral value:
      1. Particular, e.g.,
         a. That is a good car.
         b. Miniver Cheevy did not have a very good life.

2. General, e.g.,
   a. Pleasure is good in itself.
   b. Democracy is the best form of government.

B. Judgments of nonmoral obligation:
1. Particular, e.g.,
   a. You ought to buy a new suit.
   b. You just have to go to that concert.
2. General, e.g.,
   a. In building a bookcase one should use nails, not Scotch tape.
   b. The right thing to do on fourth down with thirteen yards to go is to punt.

It should be mentioned here that many writers use terms differently. Where I speak of normative judgments, some prefer to say "value" judgments or "evaluative" judgments or simply "ethical" or even "moral" judgments. For moral philosophy it is important to distinguish the above four kinds of judgments, however one labels them, and in general I shall try to use terms as indicated. Sometimes, however, especially in Chapter 6, it will be convenient to use the phrases "ethical judgments" and "value judgments" in a more general and usual way, even at the risk of some vagueness.

PROGRAM FOR REST OF BOOK

In *normative ethics* we try primarily to arrive at a set of acceptable judgments (1) of moral obligation, (2) of moral value, and secondarily (3) of nonmoral value. In *meta-ethics* we mainly seek to work out a theory of the meaning and justification (1) of judgments of moral obligation, (2) of judgments of moral value, and also (3) of judgments of nonmoral value. Chapters 2 to 5 will consist chiefly of normative ethics treated along general lines, although some analysis and clarification will come in also. Chapters 2 and 3 will deal with normative theory of obligation, Chapter 4 with normative theory of moral value, and Chapter 5 with normative theory of nonmoral value. In Chapter 6 the central problems and theories of meta-ethics will be taken up.

CHAPTER TWO

Egoistic and Deontological Theories

THE PRIMARY QUESTION

We may now begin our review of problems and views in the area of normative ethics, starting with the theory of obligation and then going on to the theory of moral value and, finally, to the theory of nonmoral value. The ultimate concern of the normative theory of obligation is to guide us in the making of decisions and judgments about actions in particular situations. A main concern, of course, is to guide us in our capacity as agents trying to decide what we should do in this case and in that. But we want to know more than just what we should do in situations before us. We also wish to make judgments about what others should do, especially if they ask us about what we or they should have done, about whether what we or someone else did was right or wrong, and so on. We are not just agents in morality; we are also spectators, advisers, instructors, judges, and critics. Still, in all of these capacities our primary question is this: how may or should we decide or determine what is morally right for a certain agent (oneself or another, possibly a group or a whole society) to do, or what he morally ought to do, in a certain situation?

IMPORTANCE OF FACTUAL KNOWLEDGE AND CONCEPTUAL CLARITY

Very often when one is puzzled about what he or someone else should do in a certain situation, what one needs is not really any ethical instruction, but simply either more factual knowledge or greater conceptual clarity. Certainly, a large part of the debate about what to do about drugs, pollution, or war arises because we are ignorant of much of what bears on these problems. On these issues and on many others, most of us would probably be clear about what should be done if only we knew all of the relevant facts. Again, in the field of education, much of our difficulty about decisions of policy is due to unclarity about what intelligence is, what liberty is, and so on. I stress these points because I think that moral philosophers cannot insist too much on the importance of factual knowledge and conceptual clarity for the solution of moral and social problems. The two besetting sins in our prevailing habits of ethical thinking are our ready acquiescence in unclarity and our complacence in ignorance—the very sins that Socrates died combatting over two thousand years ago.

Still, as Socrates' discussion in the *Crito* shows, we are often also in need of ethical guidance. A moralist might try to provide this by making a long list of specific situations, describing them and then telling us what we should do in each case. This is what is known as *casuistry* and was common in the seventeenth century. Today some philosophers seek to do something like this by discussing the ethics of abortion, civil disobedience, punishment, violence, and war. In doing so, however, they characteristically tend, rightly in my opinion, to stress general principles, careful definition of terms, and logical reasoning, rather than specific cases and detailed answers. This is the most philosophers as such can be expected to do, and it can be very helpful. In a small introductory book like this, however, we must confine ourselves to working out fairly general theories about what is right or obligatory. In fact, the best way for us to proceed in working out such a theory for ourselves is to review some of the main theories of normative ethics that have been proposed.

PREVAILING RULES AS A STANDARD

Since, as we have seen, moral philosophy begins when people find their code of prevailing moral rules unsatisfactory, moral philosophers have always been critical of the notion that our standard must be the rules of the culture we live in. To this notion, they raise a number of objections, though they do not all stress the same ones. One objection is that the actual rules of a society are never very precise, always admit of exceptions, and may come into conflict with one another. For example, the rules forbid lying and killing but do not define these terms very clearly. In fact, the rules even permit or excuse certain kinds of lying (white lies, patriotic lies) and certain kinds of killing (capital punishment, war) but they do not have these exceptions built into them in any careful way. Again, two rules may conflict in a given situation. To take Socrates' example from Book I of the *Republic,* what is one to do if one has promised to return weapons to a man who comes back for them obviously bent on harm? In such cases, two parts of the code conflict and the code often does not contain a higher rule saying which takes precedence, such as Socrates appealed to in the *Apology.*

Another objection is that prevailing rules are generally literal, negative, and conservative, not affirmative, constructive, creative, or adaptable to new situations. The most serious objection, perhaps, is the fact that the rules of a society, even its so-called moral rules, may be bad, immoral, or wrong, being unjust or unnecessarily impoverishing of human life. Rules permitting slavery and racial discrimination, once widely prevalent, are a case in point. A final difficulty, of course, is the fact that moral rules seem to vary from culture to culture.

TELEOLOGICAL THEORIES

Having agreed on one ground or another that the standard of right and wrong cannot be simply the prevailing set of moral rules, moral philosophers have offered us a variety of alternative standards. In general their views have been of two sorts: (1) *deontological* theories and (2) *teleological* ones. A teleological theory says that the basic or ultimate criterion or standard of what is morally right, wrong, obligatory, etc., is the nonmoral value that is brought into being. The final appeal, directly or indirectly, must be to the comparative amount of good produced, or rather to the comparative balance of good over evil produced. Thus, an act is *right* if and only if it or the rule under which it falls produces, will probably produce, or is intended to produce *at least as great a balance of good over evil* as any available alternative; an act is *wrong* if and only if it does not do so. An act *ought to be done* if and only if it or the rule under which it falls produces, will probably produce, or is intended to produce *a greater balance of good over evil* than any available alternative.

It is important to notice here that, for a teleologist, the moral quality or value of actions, persons, or traits of character is dependent on the comparative nonmoral value of what they bring about or try to bring about. For the moral quality or value of something to depend on the moral value of whatever it promotes would be circular. Teleological theories, then, make the right, the obligatory, and the morally good dependent on the nonmorally good. Accordingly, they also make the theory of moral obligation and moral value dependent, in a sense, on the theory of nonmoral value. In order to know whether something is right, ought to be done, or is morally good, one must first know what is good in the nonmoral sense *and* whether the thing in question promotes or is intended to promote what is good in this sense.

It should also be noticed, however, that teleologists may hold various views about what is good in the nonmoral sense. Teleologists have often been hedonists, identifying the good with pleasure and evil with pain, and concluding that the right course or rule of action is that which produces at least as great a balance of pleasure over pain as any alternative would. But they may be and have sometimes been non-hedonists, identifying the good with power, knowledge, self-realization, perfection, etc. This fact must not be forgotten when we are evaluating the teleological theory of obligation. All that is necessary is that the teleologist have *some* view about what is good or bad, and that he determine what is right or obligatory by asking what is conducive to the greatest balance of good over evil.

Deontological theories deny what teleological theories affirm. They deny that the right, the obligatory, and the morally good are wholly, whether directly or indirectly, a function of what is nonmorally good or of what promotes the greatest balance of good over evil for self, one's society, or the world as a whole. They assert that there are other considerations that may make an action or rule right or obligatory besides the goodness or badness of its consequences—certain features of the act itself other than the *value* it brings into existence, for example, the fact that it keeps a promise, is just, or is commanded by God or by the state. Teleologists believe that there is one and only one basic or ultimate right-making characteristic, namely, the comparative value (nonmoral) of what is, probably will be, or is intended to be brought into being. Deontologists either deny that this characteristic is right-making at all or they insist that there are other basic or ultimate right-making characteristics as well. For them the principle of maximizing the balance of good over evil, no matter for whom, is either not a moral criterion or standard at all, or, at least, it is not the only basic or ultimate one.

To put the matter in yet another way: a deontologist contends that it is possible for an action or rule of action to be the morally right or obligatory one even if it does not promote the greatest possible balance of good over evil for self, society, or universe. It may be right or obligatory simply because of some other fact about it or because of its own nature. It follows that a deontologist may also adopt any kind of a view about what is good or bad in the nonmoral sense.

Teleologists differ on the question of whose good it is that one ought to try to promote. *Ethical egoism* holds that one is always to do what will promote his own greatest good—that an act or rule of action is right if and only if it promotes at least as great a balance of good over evil for him in the long run as any alternative would, and wrong if it does not. This view was held by Epicurus, Hobbes, and Nietzsche, among others. *Ethical universalism,* or what is usually called *utilitarianism,* takes the position that the ultimate end is the greatest general good—that an act or rule of action is right if and only if it is, or probably is, conducive to at least as great a balance of good over evil in the universe as a whole as any alternative would be, wrong if it is not, and obligatory if it is or probably is conducive to the greatest possible balance of good over evil in the universe. The so-called utilitarians, for example, Jeremy Bentham and John Stuart Mill, have usually been hedonists in their view about what is good, asserting that the moral end is the greatest balance of pleasure over pain. But some utilitarians are not hedonists, for example, G. E. Moore and Hastings Rashdall, and so have been called "Ideal" utilitarians. That is, utilitarianism is a certain kind of teleological theory of obligation and does not entail any particular theory of value, although a utilitarian must accept some particular theory of value.

It would also be possible, of course, to adopt teleological theories intermediate between ethical egoism and utilitarianism, for example, theories that say the right act or rule is one conducive to the greatest balance of good over evil for a certain group—one's nation, class, family, or race. A pure *ethical altruist* might even contend that the right act or rule is the one that most promotes the good of *other* people. We shall, however, limit our coming discussion to egoism and universalism.

DEONTOLOGICAL THEORIES

Deontological theories are also of different kinds, depending on the role they give to general rules. *Act-deontological theories* maintain that the basic judgments of obligation are all purely particular ones like "In this situation I should do so and so," and that general ones like "We ought always to keep our promises" are unavailable, useless, or at best derivative from particular judgments. Extreme act-deontologists maintain that we can and must see or somehow decide separately in each particular situation what is the right or obligatory thing to do, without appealing to any rules and also without looking to see what will promote the greatest balance of good over evil for oneself or the world. Such a view was held by E. F. Carritt (in *Theory of Morals*) and possibly by H. A. Prichard; and was at least suggested by Aristotle when he said that in determining what the golden mean is "the decision rests with perception,"[1] and by Butler when he wrote that if:

> ...any plain honest man, before he engages in any course of action, ask himself, Is this I am going about right, or is it wrong?...I do not in the least doubt but that this question would be answered agreeably to truth and virtue, by almost any fair man in almost any circumstance [without any general rule].[2]

Today, with an emphasis on "decision" rather than "intuition" and with an admission of difficulty and anxiety, this is the view of most existentialists. In

1 *Nicomachean Ethics,* end of Book II.

2 Joseph Butler, *Five Sermons,* New York: Liberal Arts Press, 1949, p. 45.

a less extreme form, act-deontologism allows that general rules can be built up on the basis of particular cases and may then be useful in determining what should be done on later occasions. But it cannot allow that a general rule may ever supersede a well-taken particular judgment as to what should be done. What is called "situation ethics" today includes both of these forms of act-deontologism.

Rule-deontologists hold that the standard of right and wrong consists of one or more rules—either fairly concrete ones like "We ought always to tell the truth" or very abstract ones like Henry Sidgwick's Principle of Justice: "It cannot be right for A to treat B in a manner in which it would be wrong for B to treat A, merely on the ground that they are two different individuals, and without there being any difference between the natures or circumstances of the two which can be stated as a reasonable ground for difference of treatment."[3] Against the teleologists, they insist, of course, that these rules are valid independently of whether or not they promote the good. Against act-deontologists, they contend that these rules are basic, and are not derived by induction from particular cases. In fact, they assert that judgments about what to do in particular cases are always to be determined in the light of these rules, as they were by Socrates in the *Apology* and *Crito*. The following writers are or were rule-deontologists: Samuel Clarke, Richard Price, Thomas Reid, W. D. Ross, Immanuel Kant, and perhaps Butler. People who take "conscience" to be our guide or standard in morality are usually either rule-deontologists or act-deontologists, depending on whether they think of conscience primarily as providing us with general rules or as making particular judgments in particular situations.

We may illustrate these different theories to some extent by using the example of Socrates in the *Crito*. If he had tried to decide his problem wholly by asking what would be for his own good, he would have been an ethical egoist. If he had asked merely whether his escaping or not escaping would have the best results for society in general, he would have been a kind of utilitarian—what will later be called an act-utilitarian. Actually, his procedure is that of a rule-deontologist, since he simply appeals to certain rules. But, if he were to go on to defend those rules on the ground that having such rules and always acting on them is for the greatest general good, then he would be a kind of utilitarian after all—what will later be called a rule-utilitarian.

ETHICAL EGOISM

We must now discuss these various normative theories, beginning with ethical egoism, which represents one rather extreme kind of reaction to the ethics of traditional rules. This is the ethics of what Butler calls self-love and of what Freudians call the ego;

[3] *The Methods of Ethics,* 7th ed. (London: Macmillan and Co., Ltd., 1907), p. 380.

but it should be noted that an ethical egoist need not be an egotist or even an egoistic or selfish man in the everyday sense of these terms. Ethical egoism is an ethical *theory,* not a pattern of action or trait of character, and is compatible with being self-effacing and unselfish in practice. Even if an ethical egoist is consistent with his theory in the conduct of his life, he may still not do the things that we ordinarily call egotistic, egoistic, narcissistic, or selfish. Whether he does these things will depend on whether he thinks they are to his advantage in the long run, and he need not think this; in fact, he may think that modesty and consideration for others are, like honesty, "the best policy" for him to go by. He may, in other words, be quite an "enlightened" egoist.

Just what are the tenets of the ethical egoist? When he is considering the individual as a moral *agent,* he holds (1) that an individual's one and only basic obligation is to promote for himself the greatest possible balance of good over evil. What is not so clear is what the ethical egoist says about the individual as a moral *spectator,* adviser, or judge. He may say (2) that even in making second- and third-person moral judgments an individual should go by what is to *his own* advantage, or (3) that in making such judgments an individual should go by what is to the advantage of *the person he is talking to or about.* Tenet (3), however, seems to be inconsistent with the spirit of ethical egoism, unless it is based on the premise that judging as it prescribes is to the individual's own advantage, in which case (3) falls under (2). Hence I shall take an ethical egoist to be asserting tenets (1) and (2).

Ethical egoists may hold any kind of theory of what is good and what is bad, or of what the welfare of the individual consists in. They have often been hedonists, as Epicurus was, identifying the good or welfare with happiness and happiness with pleasure. But they may also identify the good or welfare with knowledge, power, self-realization, or with what Plato called the mixed life of pleasure, knowledge, and other good things.

Here we must understand that the ethical egoist is not just taking the egoistic principle of acting and judging as his own private maxim. One could do this, and at the same time keep silent about it or even advocate altruism to everyone else, which might well be to one's advantage. But if one does this, one is not adopting a moral principle, for as we shall see, if one takes a maxim as a moral principle, one must be ready to universalize it. Also, as was suggested earlier, one must be willing to see his principle actually adopted and acted on by everyone else, at least insofar as they have the ability and intelligence to do so, and even advocate that they adopt and act on it. Perhaps he need not publicly advocate all of his moral conclusions, e.g., that it is right to help slaves escape on the underground railroad; it seems to me, however, that if he is unwilling to share his basic normative premises, then he does not have a morality in the full sense. Hence, for our purposes, we must regard the ethical egoist as holding that everyone should act and judge by the standard of his own long run advantage in terms of good and evil.

Now, it has been argued that ethical egoism, as thus construed, is self-contradictory, since it cannot be to one individual's advantage that all others should pursue their own advantage so assiduously. As Kant would put it, one cannot will the egoistic maxim to be a universal law. This argument, however, does not show that ethical egoism is logically self-contradictory, for it is in no difficulty if what is to one person's advantage coincides with what is to that of all the others. If this is so, one can consistently will the egoistic maxim to be universally acted on. But, of course, this is empirically a very dubious assumption, since it postulates a kind of pre-established harmony in the world; and, if it is not true, then the position of the ethical egoist does seem to involve one in a conflict of will and thus seems to be a difficult position to maintain as a moral theory.

Partly connected with this difficulty is another. An important part of morality is the business of advising and judging. Suppose that B comes to A for moral advice. According to the ethical egoist's tenets (1) and (2), A should determine what to advise B to do by considering what is to his own (A's) advantage to have B do. Or suppose that C and D are involved in some unpleasantness with one another and come to E for a judgment between them—a moral judgment, not a legal one. Then, again, according to (1) and (2), E should base his judgment on a consideration, not of what is to C's or D's or the general advantage, but on what is to his own advantage. But surely we must regard such egoistically based advice and judgment as unsatisfactory and beside the point. It seems doubtful, therefore, that ethical egoism can serve as an acceptable basis for this important part of morality.

In any case, however, ethical egoism is advocating prudentialism as the whole story about the moral life. This seems paradoxical. For one thing, in the Judeo-Christian tradition, self-love, even of an enlightened kind, has generally been regarded as the essence of immorality, at least when it is made the primary basis of action and judgment, as the ethical egoist proposes. And, even if it be allowed that prudence is a virtue and that we do have a moral obligation to consider our own welfare, which may be debated, it is hard to believe that there are no other moral virtues or obligations that are independent of prudence or our own welfare. Here the ethical egoist may, of course, reply that he is preaching a new moral gospel, and that we cannot simply take our prevailing moral gospel as true or as a basis for rejecting his, without begging the question. The answer to this, it seems to me, is that prudentialism or living wholly by the principle of enlightened self-love just is not a kind of *morality*. As Butler said, and as Kant would have agreed, prudentialism is "by no means... the moral institution of life" even though it is "a much better guide than passion."[4] This is not to say that it is immoral, though it may be that too, but that it is nonmoral. As Butler goes on to imply, "moral considerations" are not simply those of self-love. The prudential point of view is not the moral one. The moral point of view is *disinterested,* not "interested."

If this is so, then ethical egoism, even if it involves being ready to will the egoistic maxim as a universal law (a necessary but not sufficient condition of being a moral principle, as we shall see), must be construed as a proposal to replace what we know as morality with something else, namely what Butler calls "cool self-love." Now, it may be that we should all adopt this principle of cool or rational self-love, whether as a morality or as a substitute for morality, but from what has been said it follows, I believe, that we should not do so unless there are very compelling arguments for doing so. What are the arguments that have been or may be given?

It will not do for an ethical egoist to argue that each of us should do what will or probably will promote his own greatest good because, if we do, the greatest general good will result. For one who reasons thus is basically a universalist, not an egoist. And we are interested in the arguments for egoism as a basic principle.

PSYCHOLOGICAL EGOISM

The main argument that has been used as a basis for ethical egoism is a psychological one, an argument from human nature. We are all so constituted, it is said, that one always seeks one's own advantage or welfare, or always does what he thinks will give him the greatest balance of good over evil. In Butler's terms, this means that "self-love" is the only basic "principle" in human nature; in one set of contemporary terms, it means that "ego-satisfaction" is the final aim of all activity or that "the pleasure principle" is the basic "drive" in every individual. If this is so, the argument continues, we must recognize this fact in our moral theory and infer that our basic ethical principle must be that of self-love, albeit cool self-love. To hold anything else is to fly in the face of the facts.

It is usual here to object that one cannot logically infer an ethical conclusion from a psychological premise in this way. This objection has some force, as we shall see in Chapter 6. But the egoist may not be doing this. He may only be contending that, if human nature is as he describes it, it is simply unrealistic and even unreasonable to propose that we ought basically to do anything but what is for our own greatest good. For, in a sense, we cannot do anything but this, except by mistake, and, as a famous dictum has

4 Butler, *Five Sermons,* p. 16.

Philosophy 330
Elements of Ethics
Spring 1975

Texts: Peter L. Berger and Thomas Luckman: *The Social Construction of Reality, A Treatise in the Sociology of Knowledge*

William K. Frankena, *Ethics*

Description: During the first part of the course an attempt will be made to work out a relatively systematic explanation of the process by which individuals do come to hold a given moral opinion. We will start with the basic logical features of the interpersonal situation and then move to a consideration of the individual's function within the larger social whole. Later, we will take up some typical philosophic theories specifying the moral outlook individuals ought to hold and examine them in the light of the limitations and opportunities of the actual human situation as previously worked out. In short, suggested ends will be evaluated in terms of available means. Because of the experimental nature of the subject-matter, the student's own analysis of his/her situation should provide adequate material for discussion.

Assignments: Three short (3-4 page) papers or two short and one long (6-8 page) papers on specific, assigned topics. These will be assigned at least one week in advance of the due date, and will normally be graded and returned the period after they are due. Late papers will have their grades lowered because they can take advantage of class discussion of the paper.

Final Exam: The final exam will be take-home, and will consist of two short papers as specified above. These papers [illegible] the student [illegible] learned in class.

Incompletes: Will be given only to students who complete at least two papers. They should be avoided since (a) they must be completed within the first five weeks of the next term the student is enrolled, and subsequently many students fail to complete them; and (b) experience has revealed that students who take incompletes due to laziness, moral turpitude, etc., seldom do a good job in making them up.

Instructor: Donald Koch
Office Hours: Tuesday 9-11, Thursday 2-4 in 40 Morrill Hall. As I will be unable to spend a good deal of time in the office this term, students are urged to call at home to make a special appointment.
Office Phone: 353-9379
Home Phone: 337-1834

Koch. (Coke)

...ements of Ethics
Spring 1975

...: Peter L. Berger and Thomas Luckman: The Social Construction of Reality, A Treatise in the Sociology of Knowledge

William R. Frankena, Ethics

Description: During the first part of the course an attempt will be made to work out a relatively systematic explanation of the process by which individuals do come to hold a given moral opinion. We will start with the basic logical features of the intrapersonal situation and then move to a consideration of the individual's function within the larger social whole. Later, we will take up some typical philosophic theories specifying the moral outlook individuals ought to hold and examine them in the light of the limitations and opportunities of the actual human situation as previously worked out. In short, suggested ends will be evaluated in terms of available means. Because of the experimental nature of the subject-matter, the student's own analysis of his/her situation should provide adequate material for discussion.

Assignments: Three short (3-4 page) papers or two short and one long (6-8 page) papers on specific, assigned topics. These will be assigned at least one week in advance of the due date, and will normally be graded and returned the period after they are due. Late papers will have their grades lowered because they can take advantage of class discussion of the paper.

Final Exam: The final exam will be take-home, and will consist of two short papers as specified above. These papers will require the student to utilize material learned in class.

Incompletes: Will be given only to students who complete at least two papers. They should be avoided since (a) they must be completed within the first five weeks of the next term the student is enrolled, and subsequently many students fail to complete them; and (b) experience has revealed that students who take incompletes due to laziness, moral turpitude, etc., seldom do a good job in making them up.

Instructor: Donald Koch
Office Hours: Tuesday 9-11, Thursday 2-4 in 4C Morrill Hall. As I will be unable to spend a good deal of time in the office this term, students are urged to call at home to make a special appointment.
Office Phone: 353-9379
Home Phone: 337-[redacted] 1824

it, "Ought implies can." Thus understood, the psychological argument for ethical egoism is at least reasonable, even if it is not logically compelling.

Thus, ethical egoism has generally presupposed what is called *psychological egoism*—that each of us is always seeking his own greatest good, whether this is conceived of as pleasure, happiness, knowledge, power, self-realization, or a mixed life. But must we regard psychological egoism (not to be confused with *psychological hedonism,* which we shall discuss in Chapter 5) as true? That it is true is by no means agreed on by recent psychologists, though it is asserted by some Freudians. The question is not whether egoism is strong in human nature but whether we ever have any concern or desire for the welfare of others except as a means to our own, any concern for or interest in their welfare for its own sake, which is not derived from our concern for our own welfare. In dealing with this question, I shall borrow largely from Butler, whose discussion of psychological egoism is justly famous. (1) He maintains that the desire for one's own good presupposes or builds upon the existence of more basic desires for food, fame, sex, etc. If we did not have any of these "primary appetites," we would not have any good to be concerned about; our welfare consists of the satisfaction of such desires. (2) It follows, he says, that the object of these basic desires is not one's own welfare; it is food, fame, sex, etc., as the case may be. One's own good is not the object of all of one's desires but only of one of them, self-love. (3) He adds that in some cases the object of a basic desire is something for oneself, for example, food or the eating of food. But there is no necessity about this; the object may be something for someone else, for example, that he enjoy the sight of the ocean. In other words, there may be altruistic impulses. There may also be a desire to do the right as such. Whether there are such desires or not is a question of empirical fact. (4) As a matter of fact, he goes on, there are such altruistic interests in the welfare or illfare of others (sheer malevolence, if it exists, is a desire that another experience pain for its own sake), as well as a desire to do the right as such. Our experience shows this. (5) Butler also reminds us that primary appetites such as sexual desire may even rebel against self-love, that is, may demand and obtain satisfaction even when we know this is not for our own greatest good. This is true even of altruistic impulses, for example, in cases of self-sacrifice.

At this point it is usual for the psychological egoist to say, "Yes, we do things for others, but we get satisfaction out of doing them, and this satisfaction is our end in doing them. Doing them is only a means to this satisfaction. Hence, even in doing 'altruistic' things for others, like taking them to see the ocean, we are seeking our own good." To this Butler replies (6) that, of course, we get satisfaction out of doing such things, but we do not want to do them because of the satisfaction we expect to get out of them, we get satisfaction out of doing them because we wanted to do them. The psychological egoist is putting the cart before the horse. He confuses the *object* of B's desire (A's enjoying the ocean) with the *satisfaction* that results for B when this object is attained. Suppose B fails to get A to the ocean or that A does not enjoy seeing it. Then B will experience frustration, but it will not follow that this frustration is his goal; he experiences frustration because his goal is to have A enjoy himself.

The egoist may come back by saying, "Still, I always do what I want to do, even when I do something for someone else. And the satisfaction that results is *my* satisfaction. So I am the center of it all. Egoism is still true." But if this is all that psychological egoism is claiming, the altruist has nothing to fear. For what he means by saying that there is altruism in human nature is merely that we sometimes want to do something for others and that we are so constituted as to get satisfaction out of doing so. So long as the egoist grants this, the altruist has all he is contending for, namely, that, in David Hume's words,

> . . . there is some benevolence, however small, . . . some particle of the dove kneaded into our frame, along with the elements of the wolf and serpent.[5]

Already in Butler's day, John Clarke had an answer of sorts to Butler's kind of argument. He admitted that we get pleasure out of doing things for others and out of seeing them enjoy themselves, just as we get pleasure out of eating. He insisted, however, that we get these pleasures just because of the way we are made, not because we have some prior desire for food or for the happiness of others, and that we come to desire food and the happiness of others only because we have found pleasure in these things and wish to enjoy such pleasures again. In short, one's only *object* of desire and action is pleasure for oneself. This position does sidestep Butler's argument in a way, for Butler assumes that we must first desire food or the happiness of others if we are to derive enjoyment from them, or, in other words, that pleasure comes to us only via the satisfaction of desires for other things. On the other hand, Clarke allows that we are so built as to enjoy promoting or observing the happiness of other people, and to allow this is to recognize that there is a real altruism in human beings of a kind that psychological egoists seem to wish to deny.[6]

There is more that might be said on this much-debated issue, especially because there are other kinds of psychological egoism besides that discussed by Butler. But so far as I can see, the above line of argument at least shows that we need not accept psychological egoism of the usual sort, and that the

[5] *An Enquiry into the Principles of Morals* (Chicago: Open Court Publishing Company, 1930), p. 109.

[6] For John Clarke's views, see L. A. Selby-Bigge, ed., *British Moralists,* Vol. II.

psychological argument for ethical egoism is not even psychologically compelling.

ACT-DEONTOLOGICAL THEORIES

Another rather extreme reaction to the ethics of traditional rules, but one which remains on the deontological side as against egoists and other teleologists, is act-deontologism. The main point about it is that it offers us no standard whatsoever for determining what is right or wrong in particular cases; it tells us that particular judgments are basic and any general rules are to be derived from them, not the other way around. It presents a kind of method for determining what is right, namely, by becoming clear about the facts in the case and then forming a judgment about what is to be done, either by some kind of "intuition" as intuitionists would call it or by a "decision" of the kind that existentialists talk about. Act-deontologism, however, offers us no criterion or guiding principle, but at most only rules of thumb.

If we had a distinct intuitive faculty which perceives what is right or wrong, and speaks with a clear voice, matters might still be tolerable. But anthropological and psychological evidence seems to be against the existence of such a faculty, as does the everyday experience of disagreement about what is right in particular situations. Besides, intuitionism involves metaethical difficulties, as we shall see in Chapter 6. It seems imperative, therefore, to find a more satisfactory theory, if this is possible.

The other kind of act-deontological theory, which makes "decision" rather than "intuition" central, is even less satisfactory. It leaves our particular moral judgments wholly up in the air, as existentialists think they are, subject to the "anxiety" of which they make so much. It does, indeed, tell one to take the "situation" one is in as his guide, and this must mean that one must look carefully to see just what his situation is, that is, one must be careful to get the facts about one's situation straight; but beyond that it has nothing to say, and it even insists that there is nothing else to guide one—one must simply "choose" or "decide" what to do, virtually making one's action right by choosing it. In effect, this gives us no guidance whatsoever, for merely looking at the facts does not tell one what to do if one does not also have some aim, ideal, or norm to go by. Just knowing that a car is coming tells me nothing about what to do unless I want to cross the street alive or have some notion of what I should be about. Certainly one can hardly call such unguided decisions morality. One wonders how one could even build up any rules of thumb on such a basis.

The main argument for act-deontologism, apart from the objections to prevailing rules that were listed earlier, is the claim that each situation is different and even unique, so that no general rules can possibly be of much help in dealing with it, except as mere rules of thumb. Now, it is true that each situation has something new or unique about it, but it does not follow that it is unique in all respects or that it cannot be like other situations in morally relevant respects. After all, events and situations are alike in some important respects, otherwise we could not make true general statements of a factual kind, as we do in ordinary life and in science. Therefore, there is no reason for thinking that we cannot similarly make general statements of a moral kind. For example, many situations are certainly alike in including the fact that a promise has been made, and this may be enough to warrant applying a rule to them.

On the other side, two lines of argument may be advanced against act-deontological theories. The first counts most against the more extreme ones, the other against them all. The first is that it is practically impossible for us to do without rules. For one thing, we cannot always put in the time and effort required to judge each situation anew. For another thing, rules are needed in the process of moral education. As R. M. Hare has said,

> . . . to learn to do anything is never to learn to do an individual act; it is always to learn to do acts of a certain kind in a certain kind of situation; and this is to learn a principle. . . . without principles we could not learn anything whatever from our elders. . . . every generation would have to start from scratch and teach itself. But . . . self-teaching like all other teaching, is the teaching of principles.[7]

An act-deontologist might reply that the only rules needed are rules of thumb arrived at on the basis of past experience. But this means rules arrived at on the basis of past intuitions or decisions, and we have already seen reason to question generalizations reached on such bases. In any case, it seems clear that the rules passed on in moral education must be perceived by the younger generation, at least for a time, as something stronger than rules of thumb that they may use or not use at their discretion—something more like the rules of prima facie duty that we shall come to in dealing with W. D. Ross.

The other line of argument is more technical. It holds that particular moral judgments are not purely particular, as the act-deontologist claims, but implicitly general. For the act-deontologist, "This is what X ought to do in situation Y" does not entail anything about what X or anyone else should do in similar situations. Suppose that I go to Jones for advice about what to do in situation Y, and he tells me that I morally ought to do Z. Suppose I also recall that the day before he had maintained that W was the right thing for Smith to do in a situation of the same kind. I shall then certainly point this out to Jones and ask him if he is not being inconsistent. Now suppose that Jones does not do anything to show that the two cases are differ-

[7] *The Language of Morals* (Oxford: Clarendon Press, 1952), pp. 60–61.

ent, but simply says, "No, there is no connection between the two cases. Sure, they are alike, but one was yesterday and involved Smith. Now it's today and you are involved." Surely, this would strike us as an odd response from anyone who purports to be taking the moral point of view or giving moral advice. The fact is that when one makes a moral judgment in a particular situation, one implicitly commits oneself to making the same judgment in any similar situation, even if the second situation occurs at a different time or place, or involves another agent. Moral and value predicates are such that if they belong to an action or object, they also belong to any other action or object which has the same properties. If I say I ought to serve my country, I imply that everyone ought to serve his country. The point involved here is called the Principle of Universalizability: if one judges that X is right or good, then one is committed to judging that anything exactly like X, or like X in relevant respects, is right or good. Otherwise he has no business using these words.

This point is connected with the fact, noted earlier, that particular ethical and value judgments can be supported by reasons. If Jones makes such a judgment, it is appropriate to ask him for his reason for believing that the act is right or the object good, and to expect an answer like, "Because you promised to do it" or "Because it gives pleasure." If he answers, "Oh, for no reason whatsoever," we are puzzled and feel that he has misled us by using ethical or value terms at all. Moral and value judgments imply reasons, and reasons cannot apply in a particular case only. If they apply in one case, they apply in all similar cases. Moreover, in order to give a reason in a particular case, one must presuppose a general proposition. If Jones answers your question "Why?" by saying "Because you promised to" or "Because it gives pleasure," he presupposes that it is right to keep promises or that what gives pleasure is good.

RULE-DEONTOLOGICAL THEORIES

It follows that act-deontological theories are untenable in principle. In choosing, judging, and reasoning morally, one is at least implicitly espousing rules or principles. This suggests rule-deontologism, which holds that there is a non-teleological standard consisting of one or more rules, though these need not be the prevailing ones. Usually rule-deontologists hold that the standard consists of a number of rather specific rules like those of telling the truth or keeping agreements, each one saying that we *always* ought to act in a certain way in a certain kind of situation. Here, the stock objection is that no rule can be framed which does not admit of exceptions (and excuses) and no set of rules can be framed which does not admit of conflicts between the rules. To this objection, one might say that an exception to a rule can only occur when it has to yield the right of way to another rule, and that the rules proposed may be ranked in a hierarchy so that they never can conflict or dispute the right of way. One might also say that the rules may have all the necessary exceptions built into them, so that, fully stated, they have no exceptions. Thus, for example, the case of the white lie, if we accept it, is an exception to the rule "We ought never to lie," but if we formulate the "exception" as part of the rule and say, "We ought not to lie, except for white lies," assuming that we have a way of telling when a lie is "white," then it is no longer an exception. It must be confessed, however, that no deontologist has presented us with a conflict-and-exception-free system of concrete rules about what we are actually to do. To this fact, the deontologist might retort, "That's the way things are. We can't be as satisfied with any other theory of obligation as with this one, but this one isn't perfect either. The moral life simply does present us with unsolvable dilemmas." But, of course, we need not agree without looking farther.

W. D. Ross, who is a rule-deontologist, deals with the difficulty pointed out in this stock objection partly by retorting in the way just indicated, but he also has another answer. He distinguishes between *actual* duty and *prima facie* duty, between what is *actually* right and what is *prima facie* right. What is actually right or obligatory is what we actually ought to do in a particular situation. About what we actually ought to do in the situations of life, which often involve the conflicts referred to, there are and can be, Ross admits, no rules that do not have exceptions. "Every rule has exceptions," that is, every rule of actual duty has exceptions. But there still may be and are, Ross contends, exceptionless rules of prima facie duty. Something is a prima facie duty if it is a duty other things being equal, that is, if it would be an actual duty if other moral considerations did not intervene. For example, if I have promised to give my secretary a day off, then I have a prima facie duty to give her the day off; and if there are no conflicting considerations that outweigh this prima facie duty, then I also have an actual duty to let her take the day off. Accordingly, Ross suggests that one can formulate a number of moral rules that hold without exception as rules of prima facie, though not of actual, duty. That one ought to keep one's promises is always valid as a rule of prima facie duty; it is always an obligation one must try to fulfill. But it may on occasion be outweighed by another obligation or rule of prima facie duty. Or, to use a different phrase, the fact that one has made a promise is always a right-making consideration, it must always be taken into account; but there are other such considerations, and these may sometimes outweigh it or take precedence over it when they conflict with it.

This view does much to meet the objection. It shows how we may have a set of rules that have no exceptions, namely, by conceiving of them as rules of prima facie, not actual, duty. But, of course, it does not help us in cases of conflict, since it allows that prima facie duties may come into conflict in actual situations. Ross could clear even this hurdle if he could provide us with a ranking of our prima facie duties that would always tell us when one takes precedence over the others, but he does not believe this to be possible. It is at this point that he says, "C'est la vie," and refers us to Aristotle's dictum, "The decision rests with perception." Nevertheless, as far as it goes, Ross's conception of a set of rules of prima facie duty is an important one which I shall accept and use. The main difficulty about it, besides the one just mentioned, is that a deontologist like Ross cannot give us any criterion by which to tell what our prima facie duties are, or in other words, what considerations are always to be taken into account in determining what is morally right or wrong. We must at least try to look for such a criterion. Ross simply contends that his prima facie duties—fidelity, reparation, gratitude, justice, etc.—are self-evident, so that no criterion is needed; but to anyone who doubts the claim of self-evidence, which we shall discuss briefly in Chapter 6, this explanation will hardly suffice. Other rule-deontologists would say that their basic rules are not self-evident but arbitrarily decided on, divinely revealed, or deducible from metaphysics. Such claims also raise questions about the *justification* of moral judgments, which we shall take up in Chapter 6.

Ross's standard consists of a fairly large number of relatively concrete rules of prima facie duty. A deontologist who is dissatisfied with such a scheme might, however, offer as a more satisfactory standard a small number of more abstract and highly general rules like the Golden Rule, or Sidgwick's Principle of Justice, previously quoted, or Rashdall's Axiom of Equity: "I ought to regard the good of one man as of equal intrinsic value with the like good of any one else."[8] He might then claim that more concrete rules and particular conclusions can be reached by applying these general principles. Such principles certainly capture some of the truth, for they entail a recognition of the Principle of Universalizability, but, as we shall see in discussing Kant, it may be doubted that they can actually suffice for the determination of our duties. In fact, Sidgwick and Rashdall argue that they must be supplemented by two teleological axioms—the Principle of Prudence or Rational Egoism (already discussed) and the Principle of Beneficence or Utility (to be discussed in the next chapter). Thus they come to a position much like the one I shall be advocating. Here we must notice that even if one has only a few basic axioms of this kind, one must allow that they may come into conflict (unless one postulates a divinely regulated universe in which this cannot happen, as Sidgwick does), and that one is not yet free from this difficulty in Ross's system. To be free from it we must

8 H. Rashdall, *The Theory of Good and Evil,* 2nd ed. (London: Oxford University Press, 1924), I, 185.

find a view that has a single basic principle and is otherwise satisfactory. Can we find such a view?

THE DIVINE COMMAND THEORY

A rule-deontologist can avoid the problem of possible conflict between basic principles if he can show that there is a single basic non-teleological principle that is adequate as a moral standard. One such monistic kind of rule deontology with a long and important history is the Divine Command theory, also known as theological voluntarism, which holds that the standard of right and wrong is the will or law of God. Proponents of this view sometimes hold that "right" and "wrong" *mean,* respectively, commanded and forbidden by God, but even if they do not define "right" and "wrong" in this way, they all hold that an action or kind of action is right or wrong if and only if and *because* it is commanded or forbidden by God, or, in other words, that what ultimately *makes* an action right or wrong is its being commanded or forbidden by God and nothing else.

One who holds such a view may believe that we ought to do what is for the greatest general good, that one ought to do what is for his own good, or that we ought to keep promises, tell the truth, etc. Then his working ethics will be like that of the utilitarian, ethical egoist, or pluralistic deontologist. In any case, however, he will insist that such conduct is right because and only because it is commanded by God. If he believes that God's law consists of a number of rules, e.g., the Ten Commandments of the Old Testament, then, of course, like the pluralistic rule-deontologist, he may still be faced with the problem of conflicts between them, unless God somehow instructs us how to resolve them.

Sometimes, when asked why we should do what God wills, a theologian replies that we should do so because God will reward us if we do and punish us if we do not, if not in this life then in the hereafter. This reply may be meant only to motivate us to obey God, but if it is intended to justify the claim that we ought to obey God, then it presupposes a basic ethical egoism, for then the theologian is telling us that, basically, one ought to do what is to one's own interest, adding that God makes it to our interest to do what He commands, thus leading us to the conclusion that we ought to obey God. For him, then, the basic normative principle is not obedience to God but doing what is for one's own greatest good. In short, he is a teleologist of a kind we have already discussed, not a deontologist at all. Just now we are interested only in the theologian who really believes that what finally makes an action right or wrong is simply its being commanded or forbidden by God.

It should also be noticed that a religious person who believes that God only *reveals* the moral law to a mankind otherwise incapable of knowing adequately what is right or wrong is not a theological voluntarist. He will, of course, hold that the moral law coincides with what God tells us to do, but he does not assert that what it prescribes is right just because God commands it; he may even think that it would be right anyway.

It is not easy to discuss the Divine Command theory of right and wrong in a way that will satisfy both believers and nonbelievers. The latter find the theory hard to take seriously and the former find it hard to think that, if God commands something, it may still be wrong. We must remember, however, that many religious thinkers have rejected the Divine Command theory, at least in its voluntaristic form, e.g., St. Thomas Aquinas and Ralph Cudworth.

One question that arises at once is, "How can we know what God commands or forbids?" Socrates asked this in the *Euthyphro*. However, it raises problems that cannot be discussed here. More to the point is another question asked by Socrates. Euthyphro suggests in effect that what makes something right is the fact that God commands it, and Socrates then asks him, "Is something right because God commands it or does He command it because it is right?" Euthyphro answers that, of course, God commands it because it is right, and Socrates at once points out that, if this is true, then Euthyphro must give up his theory. Such an argument does not actually disprove theological voluntarism, but it does show that it is hard to hold consistently. Euthyphro's answer to Socrates' question seems to be the natural one, and it implies that what is right is so independently of whether God commands it or not, or, in other words, that God only reveals what is right and does not make it right or create its rightness merely by willing it.

Cudworth's kind of argument is more conclusive.[9] Like others, he points out that, if theological voluntarism is true, then, if God were to command cruelty, dishonesty, or injustice, these things would be right and obligatory. If God were to order the exact opposite of what we generally take him to have ordered or of what we take to be right, then, by the hypothesis in question, this would be what we ought to do. Now, a voluntarist could reply, "So be it!" But such a position is hard to accept, and voluntarists are themselves reluctant to accept it. They usually reply by saying that God would or could not command cruelty, etc., because that would go against His nature, since He is good.

This answer may contain a circle. If, in saying that God is good, the voluntarist means that God does what is right or what He thinks is right, which is what we usually mean by being morally good, then he is in a kind of dilemma. He must either give up his voluntarism or say that God's goodness consists simply in the fact that He does what He himself commands or

[9] See D. D. Raphael, ed., *British Moralists 1650–1800* (Oxford: Clarendon Press, 1969), I, 105.

wills, which will be true no matter what He commands or wills, even if it is cruelty, etc.

To avoid this outcome a voluntarist may reply that, when we say God is good, we mean not that He does or tries to do what is right, but that He is benevolent or loving, and therefore would not order us to be cruel, etc. Such a line of thought would avoid the difficulty pointed to by Cudworth. But then we may ask how we know that God is benevolent or loving independently of knowing what He commands and whether He commands cruelty, etc., or not? To this objection a theologian may answer that God is by definition benevolent or loving, but then he is still faced with the problem of proving the existence of a Being that has the other attributes ascribed to God and is also benevolent or loving, and of doing so independently of knowing what this Being commands us to do. This problem, however, cannot be taken up here.

It may also be worth pointing out that what the theological voluntarist offers us as a guide to life is a kind of legal system, cosmic in scale and supernatural in origin, but still essentially a legal system. Since we ordinarily think that law and morality are rather different in character, we may then ask whether the action-guide of the voluntarist is a moral one at all. Theologians themselves sometimes even suggest that their religious system of life is "beyond morality" and should replace it, at least in the life of a believer. This raises the questions of what a morality is and what the moral point of view is, which we shall take up in Chapter 6, and also the question of whether God takes the moral point of view in telling us what and what not to do, which we cannot try to deal with.

KANT'S THEORY

Another example of a monistic kind of rule deontology is presented by Immanuel Kant. We must confine our discussion to what he calls the first form of the categorical imperative, "Act only on that maxim which you can at the same time will to be a universal law." In this dictum, Kant is taking a principle, very similar to those quoted from Sidgwick and Rashdall, and offering it as the necessary and sufficient criterion for determining what more concrete maxims or rules we should live by. We have, in effect, already accepted the principle as *necessary,* the question is whether it is *sufficient*. If so, our search for a normative ethics is ended.

There are problems about the interpretation of Kant, but we may take him as saying, first, that when one acts voluntarily one always acts on a formulizable maxim or rule; second, that one is choosing and judging from the moral point of view if and only if one is or would be willing to universalize one's maxim, that is, if he is or would be willing to see his rule acted on by everyone who is in a situation of a similar kind, even if he himself turns out to be on the receiving end on occasion; and, third, that an action is morally right and/or obligatory if and only if one can consistently will that the maxim or rule involved be acted on by everyone in similar circumstances, and an action is morally wrong if and only if one cannot consistently will this. Here we are concerned primarily with the last contention, though we will also have a word to say about the second. Is Kant's criterion sufficient as well as necessary for determining what is morally right or obligatory?

Let us first take an example of how he applies it. In one of his illustrations he supposes that A makes a promise but is ready to break it if this suits his purposes. A's maxim then may be expressed thus, "When it suits my purposes I will make promises, intending also to break them if this suits my purposes." But A cannot consistently will this maxim to be universally acted on, says Kant.

> ...could I say to myself that everyone make a false promise when he is in difficulty from which he otherwise cannot escape? I immediately see that I could will the lie but not a universal law to lie. For with such a law [i.e., with such a maxim universally acted on] there would be no promises at all.... Thus my maxim would necessarily destroy itself as soon as it was made a universal law.[10]

Kant concludes, therefore, that it is wrong to make deceitful promises. By somewhat similar arguments, he believes he can also show, for example, that it is wrong to commit suicide, that we ought to cultivate our natural gifts or talents, and that we ought to help others who are in trouble.

It is often alleged that Kant is being a utilitarian in these arguments, not a deontologist as he purports to be. This is a mistake. He is not arguing that one must keep one's promises because the results of everyone's breaking them when convenient or advantageous to themselves would be so bad as to be intolerable. This is how a rule-utilitarian would run the argument. Kant, however, is contending that one cannot even will such a maxim to be universally acted on, because in so doing, one would be involved in a contradiction of will; one would be willing both that it be possible to make promises and have them credited (else why make them?) and that everyone be free to break promises to suit his own purposes. In other words, he is arguing, not that the results of everyone's always acting on the deceitful promise maxim are bad, but that the results are self-defeating, since if that maxim were universally acted on, we could not even have the institution of promise making which that maxim presupposes.

It must be admitted that Kant's arguments are not always as convincing as the one against deceitful promising. It must also be pointed out that he

10 Immanuel Kant, *Foundations of the Metaphysic of Morals,* tr. L. W. Beck (New York: The Liberal Arts Press, 1959), p. 19. See selections in Frankena and Granrose, eds., *Introductory Readings in Ethics* (Englewood Cliffs, N.J.: Prentice-Hall, Inc., 1974), Chap. II.

is not free from the difficulties due to conflicts between duties; it seems possible, at any rate, that keeping a promise might on occasion prevent one from helping someone in trouble. Possibly Kant could argue in this case that it would be right to break the promise and help the person in trouble, since one can will the maxim, "When breaking a promise is required in order to help someone I will break it," to be universally acted on in the situations specified, especially if it is also specified in the maxim that the promise is not crucially important and that the help is. Kant, however, does not take this line, and talks as if he can show that promises ought never to be broken. But this his argument does not suffice to show. As was just indicated, one may be able to will a specific rule that permits promises to be broken in a certain kind of situation to be universally acted on, even though one cannot will a more blanket one to become a universal law.

Thus Kant's arguments, even if good, do not prove as much as he thinks; and in the case just presented, this is just as well, since he thought he could prove too much. Even if we admit that his criterion rules out certain sorts of action as immoral (for example, deceitful promising which does not enable one to help another), must we agree that all of our duties can be established by his test? Take the duty to help others. It is true that if one adopts the maxim of not helping others in need and wills this to be a universal law, he is likely to find himself willing inconsistently to abrogate this rule, since he is likely himself to be in need sometime. Still, it is not hard to imagine a man whose fortune is fairly sure or one who is willing to be consistent and to take the consequences of his maxim's being universally acted on; if there are such people, Kant's test will not suffice to establish benevolence as a duty. Of course, one might conclude that it is not a duty just because it does not pass this test; but this seems a drastic conclusion, and, deontological as he was, even Kant could not draw it.

Is every maxim that does pass Kant's test a duty, as he sometimes seems to think? "When alone in the dark, whistle"—this seems to be a maxim one can will to be a universal law. If not, "Tie your left shoestring first" clearly is. Yet, surely, neither of these rules can be regarded as a duty. One might reply here that such questions about whistling and tying shoestrings are not moral ones, and this is correct, but Kant does not tell us how to determine whether they are moral or not. It might also be argued that Kant was not regarding all maxims one *can* will to be universal laws as *duties,* but only holding that maxims one *cannot* will to be universal laws are *immoral* or *wrong* to act on. That is, Kant meant to say (a) that it is *permissible* to act on a maxim if and only if one can will it to be a universal law, (b) that it is *wrong* to act on a maxim if and only if one cannot will it to be a universal law, and (c) that it is a *duty* to act on a maxim if and only if one cannot will its *opposite* to be a universal law. I am, in fact, inclined to think this is what Kant meant and should have said. But even then his criterion of right and wrong is not sufficient, for it does not actually rule out all immoral maxims, e.g., the maxim of never helping anyone.

In any event, it seems to me that in order for one's maxims to be considered moral duties, it is not enough that one be able consistently to will one's maxims to be universally acted on. Much depends on the point of view from which one wills one's rules to be universally followed. One might do this from the aesthetic point of view or, more probably, from a prudential one. One might, for example, will honesty to be universally practiced because one regards everyone's being honest, including oneself (else one is not universalizing, but making an exception of oneself, which Kant is right in putting out of moral bounds), as being advantageous to oneself. "Everyone's being honest is the best policy from my point of view." If one uses such reasoning, one can hardly claim to be taking the moral point of view. There is more to the moral point of view than being willing to universalize one's rules; Kant and his followers fail to see this fact, although they are right in thinking such a willingness is part of it.

This brings us to utilitarianism, with which we shall begin the next chapter.

CHAPTER THREE

Utilitarianism, Justice, and Love

UTILITARIANISM For one who rejects ethical egoism and also feels unhappy about the deontological theories we have been discussing, the natural alternative is the teleological theory called utilitarianism. Speaking roughly, deontological theories take other people seriously but do not take the promotion of good seriously enough, egoism takes the promotion of good seriously but does not take other people seriously enough, and utilitarianism remedies both of these defects at once. It also eliminates the problem of possible conflict of basic principles. What then could be more plausible than that the right is to promote the general good—that our actions and our rules, if we must have rules, are to be decided upon by determining which of them produces or may be expected to produce the greatest general balance of good over evil?

There are less precise ways of defining utilitarianism, which I shall use for convenience, but in my use of the term, I shall mean the view that the sole ultimate standard of right, wrong, and obligation is the *principle of utility,* which says quite strictly that the moral end to be sought in all we do is *the greatest possible balance of good over evil* (or the least possible balance of evil over good) in the world as a whole. Here "good" and "evil" mean nonmoral good and evil. This implies that whatever the good and the bad are, they are capable of being measured and balanced against each other in some quantitative or at least mathematical way. Jeremy Bentham recognized this most explicitly when he tried to work out a hedonic calculus of pleasures and pains using seven dimensions: intensity, duration, certainty, propinquity, fecundity, purity, and extent. John Stuart Mill, partly in reaction, sought to introduce quality as well as quantity into the evaluation of pleasures; but, if one does this, it is hard to see how the utilitarian standard is to be stated, and Mill never did make this clear.

It follows from this understanding of utilitarianism that if there are insuperable difficulties in the way of measuring and balancing goods and evils, and there certainly are difficulties, then this fact will constitute a serious objection to utilitarianism. However, such difficulties also pose a problem for anyone who holds, as Ross and I do, that we have at least a prima facie duty to promote good or eliminate evil, and so I shall stress certain other objections rather than this one, though Chapter 5 will contain some remarks bearing on this one also.

Even if one holds, as all utilitarians do, that what is morally right or wrong is ultimately to be wholly determined by looking to see what promotes the greatest general balance of good over evil, a variety of possible views are open, and we cannot state and discuss them all. We shall distinguish three kinds of utilitarianism, each of which includes a family of views, and we must state and discuss them without attributing to them any particular theory about what is nonmorally good or bad. Some utilitarians are hedonists about this, equating the good with happiness and happiness with pleasure, and others are non-hedonists of one sort or another, but we are interested here only in their theories of obligation and not in their theories of value.

ACT-UTILITARIANISM

First, then, there is act-utilitarianism (AU). Act-utilitarians hold that in general or at least where it is practicable, one is to tell what is right or obligatory by appealing directly to the principle of utility or, in other words, by trying to see which of the actions open to him will or is likely to produce the greatest balance of good over evil in the universe. One must ask "What effect will *my* doing *this* act in *this* situation have on the general balance of good over evil?", not "What effect will *everyone's* doing this *kind* of act in this *kind* of situation have on the general balance of good over evil?" Generalizations like "Telling the truth is probably always for the greatest general good" or "Telling the truth is generally for the greatest general good" may be useful as guides based on past experience; but the crucial question is always whether telling the truth in *this* case is for the greatest general good or not. It can never be right to act on the rule of telling the truth if we have good independent grounds for thinking that it would be for the greatest general good not to tell the truth in a particular case, any more than it can be correct to say that all crows are black in the presence of one that is not. Bentham and G. E. Moore probably held such a view, perhaps even Mill; today it is held, among others, by J. J. C. Smart and Joseph Fletcher, though the latter prefers to call it "situation ethics," of which it is one kind.

It should be observed that, for AU, one must include among the effects of an action any influence it may have, by way of setting an example or otherwise, on the actions or practices of others or on their obedience to prevailing rules. For example, if I propose to cross a park lawn or to break a promise, I must consider the effects my doing so may have on other walkers or on people's tendency to keep promises. After all, even if these are thought of as "indirect" effects of my action, they are still among *its* effects.

Against pure AU, which would not allow us to use any rules or generalizations from past experience but would insist that each and every time we calculate anew the effects of all the actions open to us on the general welfare, it seems enough to reply that this is simply impracticable and that we must have rules of some kind—as we saw before in discussing act-deontological theories. But even against modified AU, which does allow us to use rules of thumb based on past experience, the following arguments, borrowed from Butler and Ross, seem to me decisive. The first is that it is possible in a certain situation to have two acts, A and B, which are such that if we calculate the balance of good over evil which they may be expected to bring into being (counting everything), we obtain the same score in the case of each act, say 100 units on the plus side. Yet act A may involve breaking a promise or telling a lie or being unjust while B does none of these things. In such a situation, Butler and Ross point out, the consistent AU must say that A and B are equally right. But clearly, in this instance, B is right and A is wrong, and hence AU is unsatisfactory. It seems to me, when I think it over, that Butler and Ross must be regarded as correct in this argument by anyone who is not already committed to AU.

The other Butler-Ross argument is that in certain situation there might be two acts, A and B, such that, when their scores are calculated, the results are as follows: A is conducive to a slightly larger balance of good over evil than B. But it might also be that A involves breaking a promise, telling a lie, or being unjust. Here the AU must say that A is right and B wrong. But again, Butler and Ross contend, B is or at least may be right and A is or at least may be wrong. Hence, AU must be rejected. There are or at least may be cases in which rules like keeping promises and not lying must be followed even when doing so is not for the greatest general good in the particular situation in question. Strictly speaking, this argument does not *disprove* AU; it does, however, make it clear, in my opinion, that AU is unsatisfactory from the moral point of view.

The point is that a particular act may be made right or wrong by facts about it other than the amount of good or evil it produces, for example, it may be wrong because it involves breaking a promise, telling a lie, or violating some rule. Butler and Ross argue thus in order to establish a deontological position, but, as we shall see, this point can be admitted and used by certain kinds of utilitarians. Much the same point has, in fact, been made recently both by deontologists and utilitarians, for example, by A. C. Ewing and R. B. Brandt. They contend that many actions that are and are ordinarily regarded as wrong would be right on an AU view consistently applied. To show this they cite cases of a poor man stealing from a rich one to feed his family, a busy citizen not going to the polls on election day, a student crossing a university lawn, a society "punishing" an innocent person to prevent panic, or a woman breaking an agreement to pay a boy for work done because she has a better use for her money. In such cases, properly hedged about, it seems clear that the act in question may produce at least as great a balance of good over evil in general as any alternative open to the agent, and that an AU must therefore judge it to be right. As Ewing puts it,

> It is indeed difficult to maintain that it cannot under any circumstances be right to lie, etc., on [act] utilitarian grounds, e.g., to save life, but it seems to me pretty clear that [act] utilitarian principles, logically carried out, would result in far more cheating, lying, and unfair action than any good man would tolerate.[1]

Of course, an AU can stick to his guns here and insist that the actions in question *are* right in the circumstances. Our question now, however, is whether we ourselves are willing to accept AU, seeing that it entails such conclusions. Like Ewing and Brandt, I am not.

GENERAL UTILITARIANISM

The second kind of utilitarianism may be called *general utilitarianism* (GU). It holds that one is not to ask in each situation which action has the best consequences, but it does not talk about rules. According to GU one is not to ask "What will happen if I do so and so in this case?" or "What rule should I follow?" but rather, "What would happen if everyone were to do so and so in such cases?" In doing this it fits in with our ordinary moral thinking in an important respect, for we do often argue against someone's doing something by asking "What if everybody did that?" with the implication that if everybody did it the results would be bad or at least worse than if they were not to do it. The idea behind GU is that if something is right for one person to do in a certain situation, then it is also right for anyone else who is similarly situated to do, and hence that one cannot ask simply what effects one's proposed action will have in a particular case—one must

1 *Ethics* (New York: The Free Press, 1965), p. 41.

ask what the consequences would be if everyone were to act likewise in such cases. This view has been best stated by M. G. Singer.[2]

It is easy to see why GU can claim to deal with the cases cited above without giving up utilitarianism. For it can allow that the poor man's act may produce the greatest general balance of good over evil in his particular situation, and yet maintain that he ought not do it because of what would happen if all the poor and needy were to steal from the rich. Here one might ask why we must always ask "What if everybody did that?" and not just "What if I do that?" The poor man, for example, might say, "I grant that if everyone in a like case were to do what I am doing the results would be bad. But in my instance it is certain that not everyone who is in a like case will do what I am doing. My action will not set an example, since others do not know about it, and it does admittedly produce a greater general balance of good over evil than the other actions open to me. Why shouldn't I do it?" The GU might then answer by pointing out that if everyone were to proceed on this AU basis, their conclusions might be misled by prejudice, passion, ignorance, and so on; but the poor man could reply once more that, by hypothesis, he is not being misled in any such ways. The GU's final answer must be an appeal to the principle that if an action is right for me to do in my situation, then it is right for everyone to do who is similarly situated in relevant respects. Now, this principle cannot be derived from the principle of utility, but is independent of it, and so one might think that in appealing to it the GU is appealing to another moral principle besides that of utility, thus giving up his ship. But the additional principle he is making use of is simply the principle of universalizability, which was mentioned earlier in our discussion of act-deontological theories, and which must be admitted by everyone who judges anything to be right or wrong, including our poor man. The real question at issue is whether the GU (or anyone else) must recognize any basic moral principle *besides* the principle of universalizability (*if* this is a moral principle, which I and many others doubt) and the principle of utility.

One might ask at this point whether GU does follow from the two principles just mentioned. This, however, is a much debated question today, and one which we cannot go into. But is the GU's answer to the poor man, the non-voter, etc., adequate anyway? This may be doubted. Cannot the poor man, for example, always fall back on a more careful description of his case and claim that the results would not be bad even if everyone situated like him, in exactly or sufficiently similar ways, were to do what he does? If so, it does not seem that the GU can show his action to be wrong. Then, either one must admit his action to be right or one must reject utilitarianism and contend, as Ewing does, that the poor man's action (or the non-voter's, etc.)

2 *Generalization in Ethics* (New York: Alfred A. Knopf, 1961).

is wrong on non-utilitarian grounds—because it is in some way unfair or unjust for an individual to take advantage of and profit by the fact that others in similar situations do not steal (or abstain from voting, etc.) or to benefit from a system of rules and cooperative activity in which he does not do his part.

Well, perhaps one can switch from GU to rule-utilitarianism.

RULE-UTILITARIANISM

Rule-utilitarianism (RU) is a rather different view, which has also been attributed to Mill and has been finding favor recently. Like rule-deontologism, it emphasizes the centrality of rules in morality and insists that we are generally, if not always, to tell what to do in particular situations by appeal to a rule like that of truth-telling rather than by asking what particular action will have the best consequences in the situation in question. But, unlike deontologism, it adds that we are always to determine our rules by asking which rules will promote the greatest general good for everyone. That is, the question is not which *action* has the greatest utility, but which *rule* has. The principle of utility comes in, normally at least, not in determining what particular action to perform (this is normally determined by the rules), but in determining what the rules shall be. Rules must be selected, maintained, revised, and replaced on the basis of their utility and not on any other basis. The principle of utility is still the ultimate standard, but it is to be appealed to at the level of rules rather than at the level of particular judgments. This view has been advocated by a number of writers from Bishop Berkeley to R. B. Brandt.

The AU may allow rules to be used; but if he does, he must conceive of a rule like "Tell the truth" as follows: "Telling the truth is *generally* for the greatest general good." By contrast, the RU must conceive of it thus: "Our *always* telling the truth is for the greatest general good." Or thus: "It is for the greatest good if we *always* tell the truth."

This means that for the RU it may be right to obey a rule like telling the truth simply because it is so useful to have the rule, even when, in the particular case in question, telling the truth does not lead to the best consequences.

An analogy may help here. On a particular occasion, I might ask which side of the street I should drive on, the right or the left. To find the answer, I would not try to see which alternative is for the greatest general good; instead, I would ask or try to determine what the law is. The law says that we are always to drive down the right side of the street (with exceptions in the case of passing, one-way streets, and so forth). The reason for the law is that it is for the greatest general good that we *always* drive down a certain side of the street instead of driving, on each occasion, down the side it seems to us most useful to drive on on that occasion. Here, for the greatest general good, we must have a rule of the always-acting kind (with the exceptions built into the rule, hence not really exceptions). If we suppose that for some reason there are special difficulties about our driving on the left, it will follow on utilitarian grounds that we should have a law telling us always to drive on the right. This, although the example comes from law, illustrates the RU conception of how we are to determine what is the morally right or obligatory thing to do.

If we ask why we should be RUs rather than AUs, the RU may answer, as Berkeley did, by pointing to the difficulties (difficulties due to ignorance, bias, passion, carelessness, lack of time, etc.) that would arise if, on each occasion of action, everyone were permitted to decide for himself what he should do, even if he had the help of such rules of thumb as the modified AU offers. The RU may then argue that it is for the greatest general good to have everyone acting wholly or at least largely on rules of the always-acting type instead of always making decisions on an AU basis. This would be a utilitarian argument for RU; and, as an argument, it has some plausibility.

RU may take various forms, depending on how it conceives of the rules that are so important in its scheme. In one form of RU, which has been called *primitive-rule-utilitarianism* (PRU), the rules simply formulate the conclusions the GU would come to, e.g., to vote on election days. It is just GU in a new dress. There is also what is called *actual-rule-utilitarianism* (ARU). It holds that an action is right if it conforms to the accepted or prevailing moral rules and wrong if it does not, assuming that these rules are those whose acceptance and observance is conducive to the greatest general good or at least a necessary condition of it. The type of RU that seems to be favored today is *ideal-rule-utilitarianism* (IRU), of which there are two main kinds. One holds that an act is right if and only if it conforms to a set of rules general *conformity* to which would maximize utility; the other that an act is right if and only if it conforms to a set of rules general *acceptance* of which would maximize utility, where acceptance of a rule is thought of as falling somewhat short of conformity to it. Of course, to make his normative ethics complete the RU must tell us which rules fulfill his stated requirements.

It has been claimed that GU, PRU, and the first kind of IRU are ultimately equivalent to AU. The argumentation here is too long to repeat and very difficult to assess, but of course, if it is correct, then these forms of utilitarianism are no better than AU. In any case, PRU is equivalent to GU and in the same boat. ARU seems questionable on the face of it, since it is very unlikely that the actually accepted moral rules of a society are all conducive to its greatest welfare or even necessary for its existence; this difficulty is compounded, moreover, by the fact that the prevailing rules vary considerably from society to society and change somewhat from time to time, so that it is hard to see how they might even be thought to maximize utility in the world as a whole. As for the two forms of IRU—there are various problems about them, but I shall try to dispose of them by stating an objection that seems to me to hold against all forms of utilitarianism, since they all make maximizing the general balance of good over evil the sole ultimate criterion of right and wrong in morality, though some do it directly and others indirectly. This objection is a generalization of an argument that has been used against AU by Sidgwick and many others.

Whether the utilitarian talks in terms of particular actions (AU), general practices (GU), or rules and sets of rules (RU), we may imagine that two of them are such that we must choose between them and such that, if we knew the results of both of them (i.e., both actions, practices, or rules), we would find that they are equal in utility, that is, they bring about the same balance of good over evil in the long run for the universe as a whole. Then the utilitarian must say that their moral score is the same and there is no basis for choosing between them. It still may be, however, that they distribute the balance of good over evil produced in rather different ways; one action, practice, or rule may, for example, give all the good to a relatively small group of people without any merit on their part (and to let merit count at this point is already to give up pure utilitarianism), while the other may spread the good more equally over a larger segment of the population. In this case, it seems to me that we should and would say that the former is unjust and wrong and the latter morally preferable. If this is so, we must give up utilitarianism in all its forms.

The point is that an action, practice, or rule may maximize the sum of good in the world, and yet be unjust in the way in which it distributes this sum, so that a less beneficent one that is more just may be preferable. For instance, it might be for the greatest general good to follow the rule of primogeniture, and yet it might be unjust to do so. If this is so, then the criterion for determining right and wrong is not mere utility but also justice. Consequently, some kind of deontological theory is the true one, for what is just is independent of the principle of utility. If justice may overrule utility on occasion, then the question of what is right cannot be answered by appeal to the principle of utility and the deontologists are correct after all, at least in part.

Utilitarians may make three replies to this argument. One is offered by John Stuart Mill near the end of *Utilitarianism.* He contends that whatever satisfies the principle of utility also satisfies the requirements of justice, since justice is built into the principle of utility.

> [Social and distributive justice] is involved in the very meaning of utility, or the greatest happiness principle. That principle is a mere form of words...unless one person's happiness, supposed equal in degree..., is counted for exactly as much

> as another's. Those conditions being supplied, Bentham's dictum, "everybody to count for one, nobody for more than one," might be written under the principle of utility as an explanatory commentary.

Here Mill is confused. It is true that the principle of utility requires us, when we are determining what to do, to count the effects of each action, practice, or rule on everyone and to weigh equal effects equally in the computation of the scores for each action or rule no matter who is concerned. But in our example, we have done all that by hypothesis and the score still comes out even. It remains true that the two alternatives distribute the same amount of good in different ways. The principle of utility cannot tell us which distribution to choose; only a separate principle of justice can tell us this.

Mill might answer that we should understand the principle of utility as enjoining us to promote the greatest good *of the greatest number,* which is, in fact, how it is often formulated. If we understand it thus, the principle does tell us that we are to distribute a given quantity of good to more people rather than to fewer, when we have a choice. The principle of utility thus becomes a double principle: it tells us (1) to produce the greatest possible balance of good over evil and (2) to distribute this as widely as possible. That is, it has become a combination of the principle of utility with a principle of justice, and to read it thus is to give up pure utilitarianism for the view we are about to describe.

The second reply has been proposed by John Laird, Ewing, and others. If we give up hedonism, they point out, we can hold that there are a number of different kinds of things that are good: pleasure, knowledge, love, aesthetic experience, and the like. We can even hold that one of the good things to be promoted is an equal or just distribution of the other things. Then when we are calculating our scores, we must figure in, not only the value of the pleasure and other such goods that are produced, but also the value of the pattern of distribution involved. This sounds like a plausible view, and it does, if accepted, take care of my general objection to utilitarianism. I find it unconvincing, however, for the following reason. As will be apparent in Chapter 5, it seems clear to me that pleasure, knowledge, and many other experiences and activities are good in themselves; but I do not see that a pattern of distribution is also a nonmorally good thing in itself. I think it may be morally *right* in itself to bring about such a pattern, however, and so I conclude that those who take the view just described are confusing rightness with goodness. Indeed, I suspect they find that view plausible only because it seems to provide a way of meeting the difficulty in question. If this is so, then their reply fails—in fact, it lends support to my contention that certain patterns of distributing things are right in themselves and not merely because of what they are conducive to.

These first two replies could be made by utilitarians of other sorts, but the third only by an RU like Brandt. He might contend that a certain principle for distributing the good, e.g., that we should distribute it as widely and equally as possible, is itself one of the rules the general acceptance of which would maximize utility. In other words, he might maintain that the necessary principle of distributive justice can itself be established by a rule-utilitarian line of reasoning. Such a reply can be satisfactory, if at all, only if it is a fact that the rule of distribution specified is more conducive to the greatest general balance of good over evil than alternative rules. This, however, cannot be shown to be a fact. If it is not a fact, my general objection to utilitarianism holds. But suppose it were the case that the rule of distributing equally, say, would maximize utility. Then RU would be saved only by a lucky fact about the world, provided, of course, that it is free from other fatal objections. This bothers me. For then the RU must say that, if the rule of distributing equally were not utility-maximizing, then it would not be valid. But this is just the issue, and to me it seems clear that the equal distribution rule would be valid anyway.

All this is not to say that RU is mistaken in thinking that such more specific rules as are usually thought of as belonging to morality can be established on its grounds, or in thinking that such rules should sometimes be acted on even when doing so does not maximize utility in that particular case. I believe that RUs and the rule-deontologists are right in holding that morality must include such rules and regard them as stronger than rules of thumb—as rules of prima facie duty in Ross's sense. This seems to me to follow if we give up AU theories (and my general objection holds against them in any case), as well as act-deontological ones.

MY PROPOSED THEORY OF OBLIGATION

So far in this chapter I have been trying to show that we cannot be satisfied with the principle of utility as our sole basic standard of right and wrong in morality, whether it is applied in AU, GU, or RU style. In particular, I have contended that we should recognize a principle of justice to guide our distribution of good and evil that is independent of any principle about maximizing the balance of good over evil in the world. It may still be, of course, that we should recognize other independent principles as well, as deontologists like Ross think, e.g., that of keeping promises. Now I shall try to present the theory of obligation that seems to me most satisfactory from the moral point of view.

What precedes suggests that perhaps we should recognize two basic principles of obligation, the principle of utility and some principle of justice. The resulting theory would be a deontological one, but it would be much closer to utilitarianism than most deontological theories; we might call it a *mixed deontological theory*. It might maintain that all of our more specific rules of obligation, like that of keeping promises, and all of our judgments about what to do in particular situations can be derived, directly or indirectly, from its two principles. It might even insist that we are to determine what is right or wrong in particular situations, normally at least, by consulting rules such as we usually associate with morality, but add that the way to tell what rules to live by is to see which rules best fulfill the joint requirements of utility and justice (not, as in RU, the requirements of utility alone). This view is still faced with the problem of measuring and balancing amounts of good and evil, and, since it recognizes two basic principles, it must also face the problem of possible conflict between them. This means that it must regard its two principles as principles of prima facie, not of actual duty; and it must, if our above argument is correct, allow that the principle of justice may take precedence over that of utility, at least on some occasions, though perhaps not always. However, it may not be able to provide any formula saying when justice takes precedence and when it does not.

Should we adopt this theory of obligation? To my mind, it is close to the truth but not quite right. Let us begin, however, by asking whether we should recognize the principle of utility at all. It seems to me we must at least recognize something like it as one of our basic premises. Whether we have even a prima facie obligation to maximize the balance of good over evil depends, in part, on whether it makes sense to talk about good and evil in quantitative terms. Assuming that it makes at least rough sense, it is not easy to deny, as pure deontologists do, that one of the things we ought to do, other things being equal, is to bring about as much of a balance of good over evil as we can, which even Ross, Carritt, and perhaps Butler, allow. I find it hard to believe that any action or rule can be right, wrong, or obligatory in the moral sense, if there is no good or evil connected with it in any way, directly or indirectly. This does not mean that there are no other factors affecting their rightness or wrongness, or that our only duty is to pile up the biggest possible stockpile of what is good, as utilitarians think; but it does imply that we do have, at least as one of our prima facie obligations, that of doing something about the good and evil in the world.

In fact, I wish to contend that we do not have any moral obligations, prima facie or actual, to do anything that does not, directly or indirectly, have some connection with what makes somebody's life good or bad, better or worse. If not our particular actions, then at least our rules must have some bearing on the increase of good or decrease of evil or on their distribution. Morality was made for man, not man for morality. Even justice is concerned about the distribution *of good and evil.* In other words, all of our duties, even that of justice, *presuppose* the existence of good and evil and some kind of concern about their existence and incidence. To this extent, and only to this extent, is the old dictum that love is what underlies and unifies the rules of morality correct. It is the failure to recognize the importance of this point that makes so many deontological systems unsatisfactory.

To say this is to say not only that we have no obligations except when some improvement or impairment of someone's life is involved but also that we have a prima facie obligation *whenever* this is involved. To quote William James's inimitable way of putting it:

> Take any demand, however slight, which any creature, however weak, may make. Ought it not, for its own sole sake, to be satisfied? If not, prove why not.[3]

THE PRINCIPLE OF BENEFICENCE

If this is so, then we must grant that the utilitarians have hold of an important part of the truth, and that we must recognize something like the principle of utility as one of our basic premises. Still, I do not think that we can regard the principle of utility itself as a basic premise, and my reason is that something more basic underlies it. By the principle of utility I have meant and shall continue to mean, quite strictly, the principle that we ought to do the act or follow the practice or rule that will or probably will bring about *the greatest possible balance of good over evil* in the universe. It seems clear, however, that this principle presupposes another one that is more basic, namely, that we ought to do good and to prevent or avoid doing harm. If we did not have this more basic obligation, we could have no duty to try to realize the greatest balance of good over evil. In fact, the principle of utility represents a compromise with the ideal. The ideal is to do only good and not to do any harm (omitting justice for the moment). But this is often impossible, and then we seem forced to try to bring about the best possible balance of good over evil. If this is so, then the principle of utility presupposes a more basic principle—that of producing good as such and preventing evil. We have a prima facie obligation to maximize the balance of good over evil only if we have a *prior* prima facie obligation to do good and prevent harm. I shall call this prior principle the *principle of beneficence.* The reason I call it the principle of *beneficence* and not the principle of *benevolence* is to underline the fact that it asks us actually to do good and not evil, not merely to want or will to do so.

It might be thought that the principle of utility not only presupposes the principle of beneficence but follows from it. This, however, is not the case. The principle of utility is stated in quantitative terms and presupposes that goods and evils can be measured and balanced in some way. The principle of beneficence does not deny this, of course, but neither does it imply this. In applying it in practice one hopes that goods and evils can to a considerable extent at least be measured and balanced, but the principle of benefi-

[3] *Essays in Pragmatism,* A. Castell, ed. (New York: Hafner Publishing Co., 1948), p. 73.

cence does not itself require that this be always possible; it is, for example, compatible with Mill's insistence that pleasures and pains, and hence goods and evils, differ in quality as well as quantity. I take this to be an advantage of the principle of beneficence over that of utility as I have stated it. There is another advantage. Suppose we have two acts, A and B, and that A produces 99 units of good and no evil, while B produces both good and evil but has a net balance of 100 units of good over evil. In this case, act-utilitarianism requires us to say that B is the right thing to do. But some of us would surely think that act A is the right one, and the principle of beneficence permits one to say this, though it does not require us to do so.

I propose, then, that we take as the basic premises of our theory of right and wrong two principles, that of beneficence and some principle of just distribution. To this proposal it might be objected that, although the principle of justice cannot be derived from that of beneficence, it is possible to derive the principle of beneficence from that of justice. For, if one does not increase the good of others and decrease evil for them when one can do so and when no conflicting obligations are present, then one is being unjust. Hence, justice implies beneficence (when possible and not ruled out by other considerations). In reply, I want to agree that in some sense beneficence is *right* and failure to be beneficent *wrong* under the conditions specified, but I want to deny that they are, respectively, just or unjust, properly speaking. Not everything that is right is just, and not everything that is wrong is unjust. Incest, even if it is wrong, can hardly be called unjust. Cruelty to children may be unjust, if it involves treating them differently from adults, but it is surely wrong anyway. Giving another person pleasure may be right, without its being properly called just at all. The area of justice is a part of morality but not the whole of it. Beneficence, then, may belong to the other part of morality, and this is just what seems to me to be the case. Even Mill makes a distinction between justice and the other obligations of morality, and puts charity or beneficence among the latter. So does Portia when she says to Shylock,

And earthly power doth then show likest God's When mercy seasons justice.

It has been contended, nevertheless, that we do not have, properly speaking, a duty or obligation to be beneficent. From this point of view, being beneficent is considered praiseworthy and virtuous, but is beyond the call of moral *duty*. All that morality can demand of us is justice, keeping promises, and the like, not beneficence. There is some truth in this. It is not always strictly wrong not to perform an act of beneficence even when one can, for example, not giving someone else one's concert ticket. Not giving him the ticket is only strictly wrong if he has a *right* to my beneficence, and this he does not always have. It may still be, however, that in some wider sense of "ought," I ought to be beneficent, perhaps even to give my ticket to another who needs it more. Kant made a similar point by saying that beneficence is an "imperfect" duty; one ought to be beneficent, he thought, but one has some choice about the occasions on which to do good. In any case, it is certainly wrong, at least prima facie, to inflict evil or pain on anyone, and to admit this is to admit that the principle of beneficence is partly correct.

A point about our use of terms may help here. The terms "duty," "obligation," and "ought to be done" are often used interchangeably, especially by philosophers, for example, in this book. This is true even to some extent in ordinary discourse. But in our more careful ordinary discourse we tend to use "duty" when we have in mind some rule like "Tell the truth" or some role or office like that of a father or secretary, and to use "obligation" when we have in mind the law or some agreement or promise. In these cases we tend to think that one person has a duty or obligation and another has a correlative right. The expression "ought to do," however, is used in a wider sense to cover things we would not regard as strict duties or obligations or think another person has a right to. Thus, it is natural to say that one ought to go the second mile, not so natural to say one has a duty or obligation to do this, and quite unnatural to say that the other person has a right to expect one to do it. This will help to explain why some assert and others deny that beneficence is a requirement of morality. The matter, it should be observed, is made all the more difficult by two further facts: on the one hand, that "right" sometimes means "ought to be done" and sometimes means only "not wrong," and on the other, that "wrong" is used as the opposite of all the other expressions mentioned, and so has somewhat different forces in different contexts.

One more remark is worth making. Even if one holds that beneficence is not a *requirement* of morality but something supererogatory and morally *good,* one is still regarding beneficence as an important part of morality—as desirable if not required.

What does the principle of beneficence say? Four things, I think:

1. One ought not to inflict evil or harm (what is bad).
2. One ought to prevent evil or harm.
3. One ought to remove evil.
4. One ought to do or promote good.

These four things are different, but they may appropriately be regarded as parts of the principle of beneficence. Of the four, it is most plausible to say that (4) is not a duty in the strict sense. In fact, one is inclined to say that in some sense (1) takes precedence over (2), (2) over (3), and (3) over (4), other things being equal. But all are, at any rate, principles of prima facie duty. By adding "to or for anyone" at the end of each of them one makes the principle of beneficence universalistic, by adding "to or for others" one makes it altruistic. What one does here depends on whether he is willing to say that one has moral duties to oneself or not. For example, does one have a moral duty not to sacrifice any of one's own happiness for that of another? We shall look at this question again later.

It is tempting to think that, since the first four parts of the principle of beneficence may come into conflict with one another in choice situations, say, between actions both of which do some good and some evil, we should regard it as having a fifth part that instructs us, in such cases, to do what will bring about the greatest balance of good over evil. This would, however, presuppose that good and evil can always be measured in some way and lose the advantages ascribed to the principle of beneficence over the principle of utility; in fact, it would make the former equivalent to the latter in practice, since we are always choosing between two courses of action, even if one of them is called "inaction." Even so, we may perhaps follow this instruction—or the principle of utility—as a heuristic maxim in conflict situations involving only the principle of beneficence, at least insofar as the goods and evils involved are susceptible of some kind of measuring and balancing, though remembering its limitations.

There are many rules of prima facie right, wrong, or obligation, to be used in determining our actual duties, which can be derived from the principle of beneficence. Wherever one can form a general statement about what affects the lives of people for better or for worse, there one has a valid principle of prima facie duty, for example, "One ought not to kick people in the shin" or "We ought to promote knowledge." Most of the usual rules—keeping promises, telling the truth, showing gratitude, making reparation, not interfering with liberty, etc.—can be seen on this basis to be valid prima facie rules. For instance, given the principle of beneficence and the fact that knowing the truth is a good (in itself or as a means), it follows that telling the truth is a prima facie duty.

Thus, some of our rules of prima facie duty follow directly from the principle of beneficence. The rule of telling the truth can probably be defended also (perhaps with certain built-in exceptions) on the ground that its adoption makes for the greatest general good—as rule-utilitarians hold.

However, not all of our prima facie obligations can be derived from the principle of beneficence any more than from that of utility. For the principle of beneficience does not tell us how we are to distribute goods and evils; it only tells us to produce the one and prevent the other. When conflicting claims are made upon us, the most it could do (and we saw it cannot strictly even do this) is to instruct us to promote the greatest balance of good over evil and, as we have already seen, we need something more. This is where a principle of justice must come in.

THE PRINCIPLE OF JUSTICE: EQUALITY

We have seen that we must recognize a basic principle of justice. But which one? What is justice? We cannot go into the whole subject of social justice here, but we must at least complete our outline of a normative theory of moral obligation, in which the principle of justice plays a crucial role. We are talking here about *distributive justice,* justice in the distribution of good and evil. There is also *retributive justice* (punishment, etc.), about which a little will be said in Chapter 4. Distributive justice is a matter of the *comparative treatment* of individuals. The paradigm case of injustice is that in which there are two similar individuals in similar circumstances and one of them is treated better or worse than the other. In this case, the cry of injustice rightly goes up against the responsible agent or group; and unless that agent or group can establish that there is some relevant dissimilarity after all between the individuals concerned and their circumstances, he or they will be guilty as charged. This is why Sidgwick suggested his formula, according to which justice is the similar and injustice the dissimilar treatment of similar cases. This formula does give a necessary condition of justice; similar cases are to be treated similarly so far as the requirements of justice are concerned, although these requirements may be outweighed by other considerations. But Sidgwick's formula is not sufficient. All it really says is that we must act according to rules if we mean to be just. Although this formula is correct as far as it goes, it tells us nothing about what the rules are to be, and this is what we want to know, since we have already seen that rules themselves may be unjust. If this were not so, there could be no unjust laws or practices, for laws and practices are rules. Much depends, as we shall see, on which similarities and dissimilarities of individuals are taken as a basis for similarity or dissimilarity of treatment.

The question remaining to be answered is how we are to tell what rules of distribution or comparative treatment we are to act on. We have seen that these rules cannot be determined on the basis of beneficence alone (as I think the rules of not injuring anyone and of keeping covenants can be). A number of criteria have been proposed by different thinkers: (1) that justice is dealing with people according to their *deserts* or *merits;* (2) that it is treating human beings as *equals* in the sense of distributing good and evil equally among them, excepting perhaps in the case of punishment; (3) that it is treating people according to their *needs,* their *abilities,* or both. An example of the first is the classical *meritarian* criterion of justice as found in Aristotle and Ross. According to this view, the criterion of desert or merit is virtue, and justice is distributing the good (e.g., happiness) in accordance with virtue. One might, of course, adopt some other criterion of merit, for example, ability, contribution, intelligence, blood, color, social rank, or wealth, and then justice would consist in distributing good and evil in accordance with this criterion. The second criterion is the *equalitarian* one that is characteristic of modern democratic theory. The third is also a modern view, and may take various forms; its most prominent form today is the Marxist dictum, "From each according to his ability, to each according to his needs." I shall argue for the second view.

Some of the criteria of merit mentioned seem to be palpably nonmoral or even unjust, for example, the use of blood, color, intelligence, sex, social rank, or wealth as a basis for one's rules of distribution. Use of ability as a basis would give us a form of the third view. This leaves moral and/or non-moral virtue as possible criteria of merit. Should we adopt a meritarian theory of this Aristotle-Ross sort? It seems to me that virtue, moral or nonmoral, cannot be our basic criterion in matters of distributive justice, because a recognition of any kind of virtue as a basis of distribution is justified only if every individual has an equal chance of achieving all the virtue of that kind he is capable of (and it must not be assumed that they have all had this chance, for they have not). If the individuals competing for goods, positions, and the like have not had an equal chance to achieve all the virtue they are capable of, then virtue is not a fair basis for distributing such things among them. If this is so, then, before virtue can reasonably be adopted as a basis of distribution, there must first be a prior *equal* distribution of the conditions for achieving virtue, at least insofar as this is within the control of human society. This is where equality of opportunity, equality before the law, and equality of access to the means of education come in. In other words, recognition of virtue as a basis of distribution is reasonable only against the background of an acknowledgment of the principle of equality. The primary criterion of distributive justice, then, is not merit in the form of virtue of some kind or other, but equality.

One might object here that there is another kind of merit, namely, effort, and that effort made should be taken as a basis of distribution in at least certain kinds of cases. This is true, but again, it does seem to me that effort cannot serve as our *basic* criterion of distribution, and that recognition of it in any defensible way presupposes the general notion that we should all be treated equally.

We certainly must consider abilities and needs in determining how we are to treat others. This is required by the principle of beneficence, for it asks us to be concerned about the goodness of their lives, which involves catering to their needs and fostering and making use of their abilities. But is it required by the principle of justice? More particularly, does the principle of justice require us to help people in proportion to their needs or to call on them in proportion to their abilities? It is wrong to ask more of people than they can do or to assign them tasks out of proportion to their ability, but this is because "ought" implies "can." Justice asks us to do something about cases of special need; for example, it asks us to give special attention to people with certain kinds of handicaps, because only with such attention can they have something comparable to an equal chance with others of enjoying a good life. But does it always ask us, at least prima facie, to *proportion* our help to their needs and our demands to their abilities? Are we always prima facie unjust if we help A in proportion to his needs but not B, or if we make demands of C in proportion to his abilities but not of D? It seems to me that the basic question is whether or not in so doing we are showing an equal concern for the goodness of the lives of A and B or of C and D. Whether we should treat them in proportion to their needs and abilities depends, as far as *justice* is concerned, on whether doing so helps or hinders them equally in the achievement of the best lives they are capable of. If helping them in proportion to their needs is necessary for making an equal contribution to the goodness of their lives, then and only then is it unjust to do otherwise. If asking of them in proportion to their abilities is necessary for keeping their chances of a good life equal, then and only then is it unjust to do otherwise. In other words, the basic standard of distributive justice is *equality* of treatment. That, for instance, is why justice calls for giving extra attention to handicapped people.

If this is correct, then we must adopt the equalitarian view of distributive justice. In other words, the principle of justice lays upon us the prima facie obligation of treating people equally. Here we have the answer to our question. This does not mean that it is prima facie unjust to treat people of the same color differently or to treat people of different heights similarly. Color and height are not morally relevant similarities or dissimilarities. Those that are relevant are the ones that bear on the goodness or badness of people's lives, for example, similarities or dissimilarities in ability, interest, or need. Treating people equally does not mean treating them identically; justice is not so monotonous as all that. It means making the same relative contribution to the goodness of their lives (this is equal help or helping according to need) or asking the same relative sacrifice (this is asking in accordance with ability).

Treating people equally in this sense does not mean making their lives equally good or maintaining their lives at the same level of goodness. It would be a mistake to think that justice requires this. For, though people are equally capable of some kind of good life (or least bad one), the kinds of life of which they are capable are not equally good. The lives of which some are capable simply are better, nonmorally as well as morally, than those of which others are capable. In this sense men are not equal, since they are not equal in their capacities. They are equal only in the sense that they ought prima facie to be treated equally, and they ought to be treated equally only in the sense that we ought prima facie to make proportionally the same contribution to the goodness of their lives, once a certain minimum has been achieved by all. This is what is meant by the equal intrinsic dignity or value of the individual that is such an important concept in our culture.

We must remember that this equality of treatment, though it is a basic obligation, is only a prima facie one, and that it may on occasion (and there is no formula for determining the occasions) be overruled by the principle of beneficence. We may claim, however, that in distributing goods and evils, help, tasks, roles, and so forth, people are to be treated equally in the sense indicated, except when unequal treatment can be justified by considerations of beneficence (including utility) or on the ground that it will promote greater equality in the long run. Unequal treatment always requires justification and only certain kinds of justification suffice.

It is in the light of the preceding discussion, it seems to me, that we must try to solve such social problems as education, economic opportunity, racial integration, and aid to underdeveloped countries, remembering always that the principle of beneficence requires us to respect the liberty of others. Our discussion provides only the most general guide lines for solving such problems, of course, but most of what is needed in addition is good will, clarity of thought, and knowledge of the relevant facts.

SUMMARY OF MY THEORY OF OBLIGATION

We have now arrived at a mixed deontological theory of obligation somewhat different from the one tentatively sketched earlier. It takes as basic the principle of beneficence (not that of utility) and the principle of justice, now identified as equal treatment. Must we recognize any other basic principles of right and wrong? It seems to me that we need not. As far as I can see, we can derive all of the things we may wish to recognize as duties from our two principles, either directly as the crow flies or indirectly as the rule-utilitarian does. From the former follow various more specific rules of prima facie obligation, for example, those of not injuring anyone, and of not interfering with another's liberty. From the latter follow others like equality of consideration and equality before the law. Some, like telling the truth or not being cruel to children, may follow separately from both principles, which may give them a kind of priority they might not otherwise have. Others, like keeping promises and not crossing university lawns, may perhaps be justified in rule-utilitarian fashion on the basis of the two principles taken jointly, as being rules whose general acceptance and obedience is conducive to a state of affairs in which a maximal balance of good over evil is as equally distributed as possible (the greatest good of the greatest number).

THE PROBLEM OF CONFLICT

Several problems facing this theory remain to be discussed. One is the problem of possible conflict between its two principles. I see no way out of this. It does seem to me that the two principles may come into conflict, both at the level of individual action and at that of social policy, and I know of no formula that will always tell us how to solve such conflicts or even how to solve conflicts between their corollaries. It is tempting to say that the principle of justice always takes precedence over that of beneficence: do justice though the heavens fall. But is a small injustice never to be preferred to a great evil? Perhaps we should lean over backwards to avoid committing injustice, but are we never justified in treating people unequally? One might contend that the principle of equal treatment always has priority at least over the fourth or positive part of the principle of beneficence, but is it never right to treat people unequally when a considerable good is at stake? The answer to these questions, I regret to say, does not seem to me to be clearly negative, and I am forced to conclude that the problem of conflict that faced the pluralistic deontological theories discussed earlier is still with us. One can only hope that, if we take the moral point of view, become clearheaded, and come to know all that is relevant, we will also come to agree on ways of acting that are satisfactory to all concerned.

The following reflection may be encouraging in this respect. It seems to me that everyone who takes the moral point of view can agree that the ideal state of affairs is one in which everyone has the best life he or she is capable of. Now, in such a state of affairs, it is clear that the concerns of both the principle of justice or equality and the principle of beneficence will be fulfilled. If so, then we can see that the two principles are in some sense ultimately consistent, and this seems to imply that increasing insight may enable us to know more and more how to solve the conflicts that trouble us now when we know so little about realizing the ideal state of affairs in which the principles are at one. Then, while Ross is right in saying that we must finally appeal to "perception," we can at least give an outline of what that perception is supposed to envision.

A PROBLEM OF APPLICATION

Another problem about our two principles may be posed by saying that they ask too much of us and tell us too little. Just look at them! One asks us to do good and to eschew and eliminate evil. But there is so much good to be done and so much evil to eliminate that one hardly knows where to begin and cannot relax once one has begun. And what about the concert ticket case? The other principle asks us to treat everyone equally. Does this mean that I must treat all children equally—that, if I pay my child's tuition, I must pay every other child's tuition? Thus one could go on, arguing that our two principles are too utopian, demanding, impractical, and unhelpful for words. This is a large topic with many facets, but one point seems clear: even if I was right in maintaining earlier that the two principles need not be supplemented by any other basic principles, as Ross thinks, they must still be supplemented in some way (even if we forget about problems of conflict between them) if we are to act on them in any sensible manner.

In answer to this difficulty I venture the following line of thought. Writers have pointed out that customs and laws may function to tell us how to do what morality asks us to do. For example, customs tell us how to show gratitude or respect, and laws show us how to provide for our children. Perhaps, then, one can argue that we need things like custom and law to help us to channel our activities in the way of applying the principles of beneficence and equality—that society must provide us with a set of mores and institutions in terms of which to operate. Take the institution of the family, for instance. It may be thought of, among other things, as directing me, say, to pay my child's tuition, and other fathers to do likewise for their children. Then, ideally, even though I do not extend my beneficence equally to all children, which is impractical in any case, all children will come out equally well treated. It still remains true, of course, that the principle of justice tells me I must treat all of my own children equally, but I need not take it to require me to do as well by everyone else's children, since the system is supposed to provide for them. Naturally, where the system fails, as it all too often does, I must still try to do something to help other children too, either directly or by seeking to improve the system.

Just what institutions society should set up is another question. I took the family only as an example. The institutions may, in fact, vary from society to society, and some societies may substitute something else for the family. In any case, however, the institutions provided by a society should themselves be beneficent and equalizing as possible. They are only ancillary and supplemental to the principles of morality, and must, as Aquinas said of human law, be consistent with these principles, even if they cannot be deduced from them.

DUTIES TO SELF

What about duties to self? Has one any *moral* duties when other people and animals are in no way involved, directly or indirectly? This again is a large and much-debated question. A great deal can be said for a negative answer to it. On the other hand, if our two principles are to be universal in scope, they must be construed as applying to myself as well as to others, so that my duties of beneficence and equal treatment cover myself as well as them. But am I doing what is morally wrong if I take less than my share? Everyone else has at least an imperfect duty to be beneficent and equalitarian in relation to me, and I have a right to my share, but do I have a duty to take it when doing so does not deprive another of his? And, if I prefer strawberry to peach jam for breakfast, is it wrong for me to take peach? I myself have much sympathy with Kant's position that one has no moral duty to promote one's own happiness, even if one does have such a duty to cultivate one's talents, respect one's own dignity, and not to commit suicide. Yet it does seem somehow arbitrary to say that our two principles must be understood by each of us as directing him to consider only the goodness of everyone else's life and not that of his own.

Once more, I venture a suggestion. It is that in theory the principles apply to everyone, that is, not only is everyone to live by them, but their scope extends to everyone, including oneself. Nevertheless, because we humans are already so prone to take care of our own welfare (even though psychological egoism is false), it is practically strategic for us in our ordinary moral living to talk, think, and feel as if we do not have a duty to do so. Kant may still be right, however, in thinking that even our practical morality should recognize such duties as respecting one's own dignity.

ARE ANY RULES ABSOLUTE?

Finally, are there any absolute rules, any rules or principles of actual duty in Ross's sense, positive or negative, that hold without exception? Kant thinks there are, but in the theory I have presented there are not, just as there are not in Ross's theory. For I have interpreted my basic principles and their corollaries all as being prima facie ones that may on occasion be overruled by others. Actually, I doubt that there are any substantive principles or rules of actual duty that ought always to be acted on or never violated, even when they conflict with others.

Here something depends on the use of terms. Is murder ever right? In a way not, since the very word suggests wrongful killing. The same is true of other words. It is better to ask if killing is ever right than if murder is, or if taking something from another without his consent is ever right than if stealing is. Then the answer is less clearly negative.

Something also depends on the kind of rules one is talking about. In the next chapter we shall find that one can speak of rules of action or doing and rules of character or being. Now, it is more plausible to regard a rule like "Be courageous" or "Be conscientious" as absolute than one like "Tell the truth." Here, however, I am concerned with rules of action or doing.

Even though I think that no such rules are absolute, as Fletcher does, I do still believe, as against him, that some kinds of action are intrinsically wrong, for example, killing people and lying to them. In denying that any kind of action is intrinsically right or wrong Fletcher is implying that killing and lying are as such morally neutral, which strikes me as incredible. They are, in Ross's terms, always prima facie wrong, and they are always actually wrong when they are not justified on other moral grounds. They are not in themselves morally indifferent. They may conceivably be justified in certain situations, but they always need to be justified; and, even when they are justified, there is still one moral point against them. Fletcher fails to distinguish between saying that killing and lying are always actually wrong and saying that they are intrinsically prima facie wrong, because he fails to see the force of Ross's distinction. Ross's words "prima facie" are somewhat misleading, because a prima facie duty, as he sees it, does have a kind of absoluteness; in a sense they have no exceptions as such—for example, lying is always prima facie wrong (always really has a wrong-making feature) and is always actually wrong unless it is made right by being necessary to avoid a great evil or by some other moral fact about it. In this sense, there are many absolute rules—our two principles and all their corollaries.

THE ETHICS OF LOVE There is an ethical theory that has been and still is widely accepted, especially in Judeo-Christian circles, namely, the ethics of love. This holds that there is only one basic ethical imperative—to love—and that all the others are to be derived from it.

> Thou shalt love the Lord thy God with all thy heart, and with all thy soul, and with all thy mind. This is the first and great commandment. And the second is like unto it, Thou shalt love thy neighbor as thyself. On these two commandments hang all the law and the prophets (*Matt.* 22:37–40).

We may call this view *agapism.* In spite of its prevalence, it is generally neglected in philosophical introductions to ethics like this, yet just because of its prevalence, it is desirable to relate it to the theories discussed and adopted here and to say something about it.

How one classifies agapism depends on how one interprets it and, unfortunately, its theological exponents have been neither clear nor of one mind about this. Philosophers, if they mention it at all, tend to identify the ethics of love with utilitarianism, as Mill did and as A. C. Garnett does. Theologians, however, would generally reject this utilitarian conception of their ethical principle, though Fletcher accepts it. In fact, it is hard to see how agapism, as stated in the above text, can be put down as a pure teleological theory at all, for, although one might argue that loving thy neighbor means promoting his good, one can hardly say that loving God means promoting his good, since he is regarded as already perfect in every respect. Only if one identifies loving God with loving his creatures, and loving them with promoting for them the greatest balance of good over evil (and both of these steps may be questioned), can one construe Judeo-Christian agapism as utilitarianism. Some Christian moralists have done precisely this, for example, the theological utilitarians who followed John Locke in the eighteenth century. In any case, if agapism is thus equated with utilitarianism, it will be subject to the criticisms previously made. Again, however, many theologians, especially today, would reject as inadequate this social gospel version of Judeo-Christian ethics.

Is their view a deontological one of some kind? Some Christian moralists have, in fact, been deontologists, for example, Butler and Samuel Clarke.

But then they have also usually held, in Butler's words, "that benevolence, and the want of it, singly considered, are in no sort the whole of virtue and vice"—that, besides benevolence, there are other valid moral principles like justice and veracity. In short, they have not been pure agapists. The same is true of the Catholics who adopt the Thomist doctrine of natural moral laws that are not derived from the law of love. Sometimes theologians have maintained that we ought to love God and our neighbor because God commands us to and we ought to obey God; or, following I *John* 4:11, that we ought to love one another because God loves us and we ought to imitate God. Then they are agapists, but only derivatively; basically they are non-agapistic deontologists, since they rest their ethics on some principle like "We ought to obey God" or "We ought to imitate God" which is taken to be more fundamental than the law of love and hence not derived from it.

It may be that we must regard pure agapism as a third kind of normative theory in addition to deontological and teleological ones. If it is not, then presumably it is covered by what has already been said. But if it is a third sort of view, it may still take two forms: act-agapism and rule-agapism. The pure act-agapist will hold that we are not to appeal to rules; we are to tell what we should do in a particular situation simply by getting clear about the facts of that situation and then asking what is the loving or the most loving thing to do in it. In other words, we are to apply the law of love directly and separately in each case with which we are confronted. This view has been called antinomianism or situationalism, and is characteristic of some religious existentialists. It is obviously open to the same objections that we made to act-deontological theories. A modified act-agapist will give a place to rules based on past experience, but only as useful rules of thumb. Fletcher's situation ethics is a modified act-agapism, but he gives it a clearly act-utilitarian and teleological twist. The rule-agapist will contend, on the other hand, that we are to determine what we ought to do, not by asking which *act* is the most loving, but by determining which *rules of action* are most love-embodying, and then following these rules in particular situations, at least whenever this is possible. For all forms of agapism, if they form a third type of theory, the basic injunction is to have a certain disposition or attitude (love) toward God and fellowman and to express it in one's judgments, actions, or rules of action.

On either view, it is not clear how the injunction to love provides us with any directive, any way of telling which act to perform or which rule to follow, unless we are to resort to the principles of beneficence or utility or to some kind of revelation (e.g., the Bible and the life of Jesus). In any case, it is hard to see how we can derive all of our duties from the instruction to love simply by itself. For example, the duty to be just seems to be as difficult to derive from the law of love as it is from the principles of beneficence or utility. The law of love also by itself gives us no way of choosing between different ways of distributing good and evil. This is recognized by the Thomist doctrine of natural law, and seems sometimes to be admitted by Reinhold Niebuhr even when he criticizes this Thomist doctrine. Emil Brunner even goes so far as to contrast love and justice instead of eliciting the one from the other. In reply, one might argue, as Garnett does, that justice is built into the law of love, since, in its second clause, it requires us to love our neighbors as ourselves or equally with ourselves. However, if we so construe the law of love, it is really a twofold principle, telling us to be benevolent to all and to be so equally in all cases. Then, the ethics of love is not purely agapistic and is identical with the view I have been proposing.

The clearest and most plausible view, in my opinion, is to identify the law of love with what I have called the principle of beneficence, that is, of doing good, and to insist that it must be supplemented by the principle of distributive justice or equality. It is, then, one of the basic principles of ethics but not the only one. If one does this, one must, of course, conceive of the principle of beneficence as asking us not only to do what is in fact beneficent but also to be benevolent, i.e., to do it out of love.

Even in saying this I am equating the law of love with its second clause. The first clause, "Thou shalt love the Lord thy God," cannot be put under my principle of beneficence. However, it raises the question of the existence of God, since we can hardly have an obligation to love God if he does not exist; and we must leave this question to the philosophy of religion. In any case, the problem of the relation between the two clauses is not an easy one. It may even be that we should regard the first as asserting, not a *moral* obligation as the second does, but a *religious* one.

Another point about the ethics of love requires mention. Its Judeo-Christian proponents generally claim that it first appeared in the world as a special revelation, that it depends in an essential way on the presence of certain theistic beliefs and experiences, and that it is available as a working principle only to those who have been reborn through the grace of God. Such claims raise interesting and important questions for moral philosophy, but we cannot discuss these here, though I shall say a little about the relation of ethics to theology in Chapter 6. Those who make such claims also seem to admit that some other moral principles are both necessary and available, independently of the law of love, for those to whom no special revelation has been made and who have not been reborn. As St. Paul says in *Romans* 2:14–15, the Gentiles who do not know the law of love still have a moral law "written in their hearts." This seems to mean that agapism cannot be the whole story. Of course, one may admit that the law of love is not the only available form of morality and yet insist that it is by itself an adequate morality, in fact, the only adequate or the highest form of morality. This, however, is true, as I have tried to show, only if pure agapism is supplemented by a principle of justice. I am even inclined to think that the life of pure love, unsupplemented in this way, is not the moral life; it is not immoral, but it may be beyond morality, as some theologians say it is.

FURTHER PROBLEMS

Here we ought to sketch a theory of moral *rights* as well as of duties, but we must content ourselves with saying that the same theory that tells us our duties will also tell us our rights. In general, rights and duties are correlative. Wherever X has a right against Y, Y has a duty to X. The reverse is not always true, as we have seen. Y ought to be benevolent to X, but X can hardly demand this as his right. In the case of most kinds of duties and obligations, however, if Y has a duty to X, X has a right to be treated in a certain way by Y. Hence, for the most part, the theory of rights is simply the reverse side of the theory of duties and obligations, and rests on the same general principles. Fuller discussion of rights must be left to social and political philosophy.

One more topic requires brief treatment here. We have been seeking the general principles for determining what is right and what is wrong. It is often said, however, that one should do what he thinks is right. We are all familiar with the following kind of situation. Smith and Jones are discussing what is right for Smith to do in a certain case. Smith thinks he ought to do X, but Jones thinks Smith ought to do Y; both present their reasons but neither convinces the other. Smith, however, is troubled and asks Jones what he should do. At this point Jones may say, "I still think you should do Y." But he may also say, "You should do what you think is right" or "Do what your conscience tells you." This suggests that we might have cut short our long exploration, saying simply "Always do what you think is right" or "Let your conscience be your guide."

Such a short way through our problem is, however, not open to us. For what one thinks is right may be wrong, and so may what one's conscience tells him. There is something that is really right for Smith to do and he and Jones are trying to determine what it is. Smith cannot determine this by trying to see what he *thinks* is right. When he thinks X is right he is thinking X is really right; but he may be mistaken in this, as he himself recognizes by talking with Jones. What is troubling is the fact that Jones says both that Smith should do Y and also that Smith should do what he thinks is right (which is X). We need a distinction here. Jones holds that Y is the objectively right thing for Smith to do, but he allows that, since Smith sincerely believes he should do X even after careful reflection, it is subjectively right for him to do X. Or, better, he believes that if Smith does X he is doing what is *wrong,* but is not morally bad or *blameworthy*—in fact, he would be blameworthy if he failed to do X, believing that he ought to do it.

It needs to be added that we do not and can not always regard an agent as free from blame when he does what he thinks is right. We do not and cannot simply excuse the Nazis for their crimes against humanity even if we think they sincerely believed that what they were doing was right, partly because the wrong is too heinous and partly because a man may be responsible for his moral errors.

It remains true, nevertheless, that a man must in the moment of decision do what he thinks is right. He cannot do otherwise. This does not mean that what he does will be right or even that he will not be worthy of blame or punishment. He simply has no choice, for he cannot at that moment see any discrepancy between what is right and what he thinks is right. He cannot be morally good if he does not do what he finally believes to be right, but even then, what he does may not be what he ought to do. The life of man, even if he would be moral, is not without its risks.

Some relativists insist, of course, that there is no such thing as something it is objectively right to do, that there is no distinction between what is (really) right and what one thinks is right. In actual moral living, however, a man must make such a distinction. Else he cannot even have a question to ask about what he should do.

CHAPTER FOUR

Moral Value and Responsibility

We have been a long time considering the central question of normative ethics, namely, that of the basic principles, criteria, or standards by which we are to determine what we morally ought to do, what is morally right or wrong, and what our moral rights are. We saw earlier, however, that there are other moral judgments besides deontic judgments in which we say of actions or kinds of action that they are right, wrong, or obligatory, namely, aretaic judgments in which we say of persons, traits of character, motives, intentions, etc., and also of "deeds," that they are morally good or bad, responsible, blameworthy or praiseworthy, admirable or despicable, heroic or saintly, virtuous or vicious, etc. We must, then, say something about the question on what basis or by what standard we should make such judgments. In other words, we must have a normative theory of moral value to supplement our normative theory of moral obligation, even though we can give relatively little space or time to working one out.

MORAL AND NONMORAL SENSES OF "GOOD"

Moral value (moral goodness and badness) must be distinguished, not only from moral obligatoriness, rightness, and wrongness, but also from nonmoral value. Moral values or things that are morally good must be distinguished from nonmoral values or things that are good in a nonmoral sense. We must, therefore, say a little more than we did in Chapter 1 about the latter distinction. Partly, it is a matter of the difference in the *objects* that are called good or bad. The sorts of things that may be morally good or bad are persons, groups of persons, traits of character, dispositions, emotions, motives, and intentions—in short, persons, groups of persons, and elements of personality. All sorts of things, on the other hand, may be nonmorally good or bad, for example: physical objects like cars and paintings; experiences like pleasure, pain, knowledge, and freedom; and forms of government like democracy. It does not make sense to call most of these things morally good or bad, unless we mean that it is morally right or wrong to pursue them. Partly, the distinction between judgments of moral and nonmoral value is also a matter of the difference in the *grounds* on or *reasons* for which they are made. When we judge actions or persons to be morally good or bad we always do so because of the motives, intentions, dispositions, or traits of character they manifest. When we make nonmoral judgments it is on very different grounds or reasons, and the grounds or reasons vary from case to case, depending, for example, on whether our judgment is one of intrinsic, instrumental, or aesthetic value.

Of course, the same thing may be both morally good and nonmorally good. Love of fellow man is a morally good disposition or emotion; it is normally also a source of happiness and so is good in a nonmoral sense. But the ground or reason for its being good is different in the two judgments. Consider also the expressions "a good life" and "the good life." We sometimes say of a man that he "*had* a good life"; we also sometimes say that he "*led* a good life." In both cases we are saying that his life was good; but in the second case we are saying that it was morally good, or useful, or virtuous, while in the first we are saying, in effect, that it was happy or satisfying, that is, that it was good but in a nonmoral sense (which, again, is not to say that it was immoral). It will, therefore, be convenient for our purposes to speak of "the morally good life" on the one hand, and of "the nonmorally good life" on the other. Since the latter expression seems rather odd, I shall hereafter use the phrase "the good life" to mean the nonmorally good life, especially in Chapter 5.

MORALITY AND CULTIVATION OF TRAITS

Our present interest, then, is not in moral principles nor in nonmoral values, but in moral values, in what is morally good or bad. Throughout its history morality has been concerned about the cultivation of certain dispositions, or traits, among which are "character" and such "virtues" (an old-fashioned but still useful term) as honesty, kindness, and conscientiousness. Virtues are dispositions or traits that are not wholly innate; they must all be acquired, at least in part, by teaching and practice, or, perhaps, by grace. They are also traits of "character," rather than traits of "personality" like charm or shyness, and they all involve a tendency to do certain kinds of action in certain kinds of situations, not just to think or feel in certain ways. They are not just abilities or skills, like intelligence or carpentry, which one may have without using.

In fact, it has been suggested that morality is or should be conceived as primarily concerned, not with rules or principles as we have been supposing so far, but with the cultivation of such dispositions or traits of character. Plato and Aristotle seem to conceive of morality in this way, for they talk mainly in terms of virtues and the virtuous, rather than in terms of what is right or obligatory. Hume uses similar terms, although he mixes in some nonmoral traits like cheerfulness and wit along with moral ones like benevolence and justice. More recently, Leslie Stephen stated the view in these words:

> ...morality is internal. The moral law...has to be expressed in the form, "be this," not in the form, "do this." ...the true moral law says "hate not," instead of "kill not."... the only mode of stating the moral law must be as a rule of character.[1]

ETHICS OF VIRTUE

Those who hold this view are advocating an *ethics of virtue* or being, in opposition to an ethics of duty, principle, or doing, and we should note here that, although the ethical theories criticized or defended in Chapters 2 and 3 were all stated as kinds of ethics of duty, they could also be recast as kinds of ethics of virtue. The notion of an ethics of virtue is worth looking at here, not only because it has a long history but also because some spokesmen of "the new morality" seem to espouse it. What would an ethics of virtue be like? It would, of course, not take deontic judgments or principles as basic in morality, as we have been doing; instead, it would take as basic aretaic judgments like "That was a courageous deed," "His action was virtuous," or "Courage is a virtue," and it would insist that deontic judgments are either derivative from such aretaic ones or can be dispensed with entirely. Moreover, it would regard aretaic judgments about actions as secondary and as based on aretaic judgments about agents and their motives or traits, as Hume does when he writes:

> ...when we praise any actions, we regard only the motives that produced them.... The external performance has no merit.... all virtuous actions derive their merit only from virtuous motives.[2]

For an ethics of virtue, then, what is basic in morality is judgments like "Benevolence is a good motive," "Courage is a virtue," "The morally good

1 *The Science of Ethics* (New York: G. P. Putnam's Sons, 1882), pp. 155, 158.

2 *Treatise of Human Nature,* Book III, Part II, opening of Sec. I.

man is kind to everyone" or, more simply and less accurately, "Be loving!"—not judgments or principles about what our duty is or what we ought to do. But, of course, it thinks that its basic instructions will guide us, not only about what to be, but also about what to do.

It looks as if there would be three kinds of ethics of virtue, corresponding to the three kinds of ethics of duty covered earlier. The question to be answered is: What dispositions or traits are moral virtues? *Trait-egoism* replies that the virtues are the dispositions that are most conducive to one's own good or welfare, or, alternatively, that prudence or a careful concern for one's own good is the cardinal or basic moral virtue, other virtues being derivative from it. *Trait-utilitarianism* asserts that the virtues are those traits that most promote the general good, or, alternatively, that benevolence is the basic or cardinal moral virtue. These views may be called *trait-teleological,* but, of course, there are also *trait-deontological theories,* which will hold that certain traits are morally good or virtuous simply as such, and not just because of the nonmoral value they may have or promote, or, alternatively, that there are other cardinal or basic virtues besides prudence or benevolence, for example, obedience to God, honesty, or justice. If they add that there is only one such cardinal virtue, they are monistic, otherwise pluralistic.

To avoid confusion, it is necessary to notice here that we must distinguish between *virtues* and *principles of duty* like "We ought to promote the good" and "We ought to treat people equally." A virtue is not a principle of this kind; it is a disposition, habit, quality, or trait of the person or soul, which an individual either has or seeks to have. Hence, I speak of the principle of *beneficence* and the virtue of *benevolence,* since we have two words with which to mark the difference. In the case of justice, we do not have different words, but still we must not confuse the principle of equal treatment with the disposition to treat people equally.

On the basis of our earlier discussions, we may assume at this point that views of the first two kinds are unsatisfactory, and that the most adequate ethics of virtue would be one of the third sort, one that would posit two cardinal virtues, namely, benevolence and justice, considered now as dispositions or traits of character rather than as principles of duty. By a set of cardinal virtues is meant a set of virtues such that (1) they cannot be derived from one another and (2) all other moral virtues can be derived from or shown to be forms of them. Plato and other Greeks thought there were four cardinal virtues in this sense: wisdom, courage, temperance, and justice. Christianity is traditionally regarded as having seven cardinal virtues: three "theological" virtues—faith, hope, and love; and four "human" virtues—prudence, fortitude, temperance, and justice. This was essentially St. Thomas Aquinas's view; since St. Augustine regarded the last four as forms of love, only the first three were really cardinal for him. However, many moralists, among them Schopenhauer, have taken benevolence and justice to be the cardinal moral virtues, as I would. It seems to me that all of the usual virtues (such as love, courage, temperance, honesty, gratitude, and considerateness), at least insofar as they are *moral* virtues, can be derived from these two. Insofar as a disposition cannot be derived from benevolence and justice, I should try to argue either that it is not a *moral* virtue (e.g., I take faith, hope, and wisdom to be religious or intellectual, not moral, virtues) or that it is not a virtue at all.

ON BEING AND DOING: MORALITY OF TRAITS VS. MORALITY OF PRINCIPLES

We may now return to the issue posed by the quotation from Stephen, though we cannot debate it as fully as we should.[3] To be or to do, that is the question. Should we construe morality as primarily a following of certain principles or as primarily a cultivation of certain dispositions and traits? Must we choose? It is hard to see how a morality of principles can get off the ground except through the development of dispositions to act in accordance with its principles, else all motivation to act on them must be of an *ad hoc* kind, either prudential or impulsively altruistic. Moreover, morality can hardly be content with a mere conformity to rules, however willing and self-conscious it may be, unless it has no interest in the spirit of its law but only in the letter. On the other hand, one cannot conceive of traits of character except as including dispositions and tendencies to act in certain ways in certain circumstances. Hating involves being disposed to kill or harm, being just involves tending to do just acts (acts that conform to the principle of justice) when the occasion calls. Again, it is hard to see how we could know what traits to encourage or inculcate if we did not subscribe to principles, for example, to the principle of utility, or to those of benevolence and justice.

I propose therefore that we regard the morality of duty and principles and the morality of virtues or traits of character not as rival kinds of morality between which we must choose, but as two complementary aspects of the same morality. Then, for every principle there will be a morally good trait, often going by the same name, consisting of a disposition or tendency to act according to it; and for every morally good trait there will be a principle defining the kind of action in which it is to express itself. To parody a famous dictum of Kant's, I am inclined to think that principles without traits are impotent and traits without principles are blind.

Even if we adopt this double-aspect conception of morality, in which

3 For a fuller discussion see my "Prichard and the Ethics of Virtue," *Monist* (1971), 54, 1–17.

principles are basic, we may still agree that morality does and must put a premium on *being* honest, conscientious, and so forth. If its sanctions or sources of motivation are not to be entirely external (for example, the prospect of being praised, blamed, rewarded, or punished by others) or adventitious (for example, a purely instinctive love of others), if it is to have adequate "internal sanctions," as Mill called them, then morality must foster the development of such dispositions and habits as have been mentioned. It could hardly be satisfied with a mere conformity to its principles even if it could provide us with fixed principles of actual duty. For such a conformity might be motivated entirely by extrinsic or nonmoral considerations, and would then be at the mercy of these other considerations. It could not be counted on in a moment of trial. Besides, since morality cannot provide us with fixed principles of actual duty but only with principles of prima facie duty, it cannot be content with the letter of its law, but must foster in us the dispositions that will sustain us in the hour of decision when we are choosing between conflicting principles of prima facie duty or trying to revise our working rules of right and wrong.

There is another reason why we must cultivate certain traits of character in ourselves and others, or why we must be certain sorts of persons. Although morality is concerned that we act in certain ways, it cannot take the hard line of insisting that we act in precisely those ways, even if those ways could be more clearly defined. We cannot praise and blame or apply other sanctions to an agent simply on the ground that he has or has not acted in conformity with certain principles. It would not be right. Through no fault of his own, the agent may not have known all the relevant facts. What action the principles of morality called for in the situation may not have been clear to him, again through no fault of his own, and he may have been honestly mistaken about his duty. Or his doing what he ought to have done might have carried with it an intolerable sacrifice on his part. He may even have been simply incapable of doing it. Morality must therefore recognize various sorts of excuses and extenuating circumstances. All it can really insist on, then, except in certain critical cases, is that we develop and manifest fixed dispositions to find out what the right thing is and to do it if possible. In this sense a person must "be this" rather than "do this." But it must be remembered that "being" involves at least *trying* to "do." Being without doing, like faith without works, is dead.

At least it will be clear from this discussion that an ethics of duty or principles also has an important place for the virtues and must put a premium on their cultivation as a part of moral education and development. The place it has for virtue and/or the virtues is, however, different from that accorded them by an ethics of virtue. Talking in terms of the theory defended in Chapter 3, which was an ethics of duty, we may say that, if we ask for *guidance* about what to do or not do, then the answer is contained, at least primarily, in two deontic principles and their corollaries, namely, the principles of beneficence and equal treatment. Given these two deontic principles, plus the necessary clarity of thought and factual knowledge, we can know what we morally ought to do or not do, except perhaps in cases of conflict between them. We also know that we should cultivate two virtues, a disposition to be beneficial (i.e., benevolence) and a disposition to treat people equally (justice as a trait). But the point of acquiring these virtues is not further guidance or instruction; the function of the virtues in an ethics of duty is not to tell us what to do but to ensure that we will do it willingly in whatever situations we may face. In an ethics of virtue, on the other hand, the virtues play a dual role—they must not only move us to do what we do, they must also tell us what to do. To parody Alfred Lord Tennyson:

Theirs not (only) to do or die,
Theirs (also) to reason why.

MORAL IDEALS This is the place to mention ideals again, which are among what we called the ingredients of morality. One may, perhaps, identify moral ideals with moral principles, but, more properly speaking, moral ideals are ways of being rather than of doing. Having a moral ideal is wanting to be a person of a certain sort, wanting to have a certain trait of character rather than others, for example, moral courage or perfect integrity. That is why the use of exemplary persons like Socrates, Jesus, or Martin Luther King has been such an important part of moral education and self-development, and it is one of the reasons for the writing and reading of biographies or of novels and epics in which types of moral personality are portrayed, even if they are not all heroes or saints. Often such moral ideals of personality go beyond what can be demanded or regarded as obligatory, belonging among the things to be praised rather than required, except as one may require them of oneself. It should be remembered, however, that not all personal ideals are moral ones. Achilles, Hercules, Napoleon, and Prince Charming may all be taken as ideals, but the ideals they represent are not moral ones, even though they may not be immoral ones either. Some ideals, e.g., those of chivalry, may be partly moral and partly nonmoral. There is every reason why one should pursue nonmoral as well as moral ideals, but there is no good reason for confusing them.

When one has a moral ideal, wanting to be a certain sort of moral person, one has at least some motivation to live in a certain way, but one also has something to guide him in living. Here the idea of an ethics of virtue may have a point. One may, of course, take as one's ideal that of being a good man who always does his duty from a sense of duty, perhaps gladly, and perhaps even going a second mile on occasion. Then one's guidance clearly comes entirely from one's rules and principles of duty. However, one may also have an ideal that goes beyond anything that can be regarded by others or even oneself as strict duty or obligation, a form or style of personal being that may be morally good or virtuous, but is not morally required of one. An ethics of virtue seems to provide for such an aspiration more naturally than an ethics of duty or principle, and perhaps an adequate morality should at least contain a region in which we can follow such an ideal, over and beyond the region in which we are to listen to the call of duty. There certainly should be moral heroes and saints who go beyond the merely good man, if only to serve as an inspiration to others to be better and do more than they would otherwise be or do. Granted all this, however, it still seems to me that, if one's ideal is truly a moral one, there will be nothing in it that is not covered by the principles of beneficence and justice conceived as principles of what we ought to do in the wider sense referred to earlier.

DISPOSITIONS TO BE CULTIVATED

Are there any other moral virtues to be cultivated besides benevolence and justice? No cardinal ones, of course. In this sense our answer to Socrates' question whether virtue is one or many is that it is two. We saw, however, that the principles of beneficence and equality have corollaries like telling the truth, keeping promises, etc. It follows that character traits like honesty and fidelity are virtues, though subordinate ones, and should be acquired and fostered. There will then be other such virtues corresponding to other corollaries of our main principles. Let us call all of these virtues, cardinal and non-cardinal, first-order moral virtues. Besides first-order virtues like these, there are certain other moral virtues that ought also to be cultivated, which are in a way more abstract and general and may be called second-order virtues. Conscientiousness is one such virtue; it is not limited to a certain sector of the moral life, as gratitude and honesty are, but is a virtue covering the whole of the moral life. Moral courage, or courage when moral issues are at stake, is another such second-order virtue; it belongs to all sectors of the moral life. Others that overlap with these are integrity and good-will, understanding good-will in Kant's sense of respect for the moral law.

In view of what was said in a previous chapter, we must list two other second-order traits: a disposition to find out and respect the relevant facts and a disposition to think clearly. These are not just abilities but character traits; one might have the ability to think intelligently without having a disposition to use it. They are therefore virtues, though they are intellectual virtues, not moral ones. Still, though their role is not limited to the moral life, they are necessary to it. More generally speaking, we should cultivate the virtue Plato called wisdom and Aristotle practical wisdom, which they thought of as including all of the intellectual abilities and virtues essential to the moral life.

Still other second-order qualities, which may be abilities rather than virtues, but which must be cultivated for moral living, and so may, perhaps, best be mentioned here, are moral autonomy, the ability to make moral decisions and to revise one's principles if necessary, and the ability to realize vividly, in imagination and feeling, the "inner lives" of others. Of these second-order qualities, the first two have been referred to on occasion and will be again, but something should be said about the last.

If our morality is to be more than a conformity to internalized rules and principles, if it is to include and rest on an understanding of the point of these rules and principles, and certainly if it is to involve *being* a certain kind of person and not merely *doing* certain kinds of things, then we must somehow attain and develop an ability to be aware of others as persons, as important to themselves as we are to ourselves, and to have a lively and sympathetic representation in imagination of their interests and of the effects of our actions on their lives. The need for this is particularly stressed by Josiah Royce and William James. Both men point out how we usually go our own busy and self-concerned ways, with only an external awareness of the presence of others, much as if they were things, and without any realization of their inner and peculiar worlds of personal experience; and both emphasize the need and the possibility of a "higher vision of an inner significance" which pierces this "certain blindness in human beings" and enables us to realize the existence of others in a wholly different way, as we do our own.

> What then is thy neighbor? He too is a mass of states, of experiences, thoughts and desires, just as concrete, as thou art. . . . Dost thou believe this? Art thou sure what it means? This is for thee the turning-point of thy whole conduct towards him.[4]

These are Royce's quaint old-fashioned words. Here are James's more modern ones.

> This higher vision of an inner significance in what, until then, we had realized only in the dead external way, often comes over a person suddenly; and, when it does so, it makes an epoch in his history.[5]

Royce calls this more perfect recognition of our neighbors "the moral insight" and James says that its practical consequence is "the well-known democratic respect for the sacredness of individuality." It is hard to see how either a benevolent (loving) or a just (equalitarian) disposition could come to fruition without it. To quote James again,

[4] *The Religious Aspect of Philosophy* (New York: Harper & Row, Publishers, 1958), Harper Torchbook edition, pp. 156–57. See selections in Frankena and Granrose, Chap. IV.

[5] *On Some of Life's Ideals* (New York: Holt, Rinehart and Winston, Inc., 1899), p. 20.

We ought, all of us, to realize each other in this intense, pathetic, and important way.[6]

Doing this is part of what is involved in fully taking the moral point of view.

TWO QUESTIONS We can now deal with the question, sometimes raised, whether an action is to be judged right or wrong because of its results, because of the principle it exemplifies, or because the motive, intention, or trait of character involved is morally good or bad. The answer, implied in what was said in Chapters 2 and 3, is that an action is to be judged *right* or *wrong* by reference to a principle or set of principles. Even if we say it is right or wrong because of its effects, this means that it is right or wrong by the principle of utility or some other teleological principle. But an act may also be said to be *good* or *bad,* praiseworthy or blameworthy, noble or despicable, and so on, and then the moral quality ascribed to it will depend on the agent's motive, intention, or disposition in doing it.

Another important question here is: What is moral goodness? When is a person morally good and when are his actions, dispositions, motives, or intentions morally good? Not just when he does what is actually right, for he may do what is right from bad motives, in which case he is not morally good, or he may fail to do what is right though sincerely trying to do it, in which case he is not morally bad. Whether he and his actions are morally good or not depends, not on the rightness of what he does or on its consequences, but on his character or motives; so far the statement quoted from Hume is certainly correct. But when are his motives and dispositions morally good? Some answer that a person and his actions are morally good if and only if they are motivated wholly by a sense of duty or a desire to do what is right; the Stoics and Kant sometimes seem to take this extreme view. Others hold that a man and his actions are morally good if and only if they are motivated primarily by a sense of duty or desire to do what is right, though other motives may be present too; still others contend, with Aristotle, that they are at any rate not morally good unless they are motivated at least in part by such a sense or desire. A more reasonable view, to my mind, is that a man and his actions are morally good if it is at least true that, whatever his actual motives in acting are, his sense of duty or desire to do the right is so strong in him that it would keep him trying to do his duty anyway.

Actually, I find it hard to believe that no dispositions or motivations are good or virtuous from the moral point of view except those that include a will to do the right as such. It is more plausible to distinguish two kinds of morally good dispositions or traits of character, first, those that are usually called moral virtues and do include a will to do the right, and second, others

6 *Life's Ideals,* p. 51.

like purely natural kindliness or gratefulness, which, while they are nonmoral, are still morality-supporting, since they dispose us to do such actions as morality requires and even to perform deeds, for example, in the case of motherly love, which are well beyond the call of duty.

It has even been alleged that conscientiousness or moral goodness in the sense of a disposition to act from a sense of duty alone is not a good thing or not a virtue—that it is more desirable to have people acting from motives like friendship, gratitude, honor, love, and the like, than from a dry or driven sense of obligation. There is something to be said for this view, though it ignores the nobility of great moral courage and of the higher reaches of moral idealism. But even if conscientiousness or good will is not the only thing that is unconditionally good, as Kant believed, or the greatest of intrinsically good things, as Ross thought, it is surely a good thing from the moral point of view. For an ethics of duty, at any rate, it must be desirable that people do what is right for its own sake, especially if they do it gladly, as a gymnast may gladly make the right move just because it is right.

MORAL RESPONSIBILITY

There are many other questions and topics that should be taken up here, but we can deal with only one of them—that of moral responsibility. In one of our many kinds of moral judgments, we attribute moral responsibility to certain agents. There are at least three kinds of cases in which we do this. (1) We sometimes say, in recommending X, that he is responsible or is a responsible person, meaning to say something morally favorable about his character. (2) We also say, where Y is a past action or crime, that X was and is responsible for it. (3) Finally, we say that X is responsible for Y, where Y is something still to be done, meaning that he has the responsibility for doing it.

Here, saying that X is responsible in the first sense is roughly equivalent to saying that X can be counted on to carry out his responsibilities in the third sense; responsibility of this first sort is another of the second-order virtues we should try to cultivate. To say that X has certain responsibilities in the third sense is simply to say that he has obligations, either because of his office or because of his previous commitments to do certain things, and hence is a straight normative judgment of obligation. The most interesting new problem comes up in connection with ascriptions of responsibility of the second kind. Under what conditions is it correct or right to judge or say that X was responsible for Y?

Saying that X was responsible for Y seems, at first, to be a causal, not a moral, judgment; and one might, therefore, be inclined to say that "X was responsible for Y" simply means "X caused Y," perhaps with the qualification that he did so voluntarily, intentionally, etc. But to say that X was responsible for Y is not merely to make a causal statement of a special kind.

Neither is it simply a statement that X was *able* to do Y, as the "ible" ending suggests. Suffixes like "ible" and "able" do not always indicate an ability. They may have a normative meaning. Mill's critics have often criticized his argument that the way to prove something is desirable is to show it is desired, just as the way to prove something is audible is to prove it is heard. They point out, quite rightly, that "desirable" does not mean "can be desired" as "audible" means "can be heard"; rather it means something like "good" or "ought to be desired." Similarly, it seems to me, to say that X was responsible for Y is to say something like "It would be right to hold X responsible for Y and to blame or otherwise punish him." Or, perhaps, saying that X was responsible for Y under certain conditions is simply one way of holding him responsible. In the former case, it is a normative judgment; in the latter, it is a kind of act, like making an assignment. In either case, it is not a causal statement even of a special sort. But in either case, we may ask under what conditions it is right to ascribe responsibility to X.

It seems clear at once that one of the conditions required is that X was *able* to do it and another is that he, in fact, *did* it (i.e., caused it voluntarily, intentionally, etc.). These are necessary conditions of his being responsible or being held responsible. Are they sufficient?

Aristotle held, in effect, that an individual is responsible for his act if and only if (1) its cause is internal to him, i.e., he is not compelled to act by someone or something external to him, and (2) his doing it is not a result of any ignorance he has not brought about by his own previous choices. Then and only then can his action be said to be "voluntary." These two conditions are clearly among those necessary for responsibility; we may, in fact, understand them to be included in the second of the conditions just listed. Are there any others? G. E. Moore, P. H. Nowell-Smith, and others have held that a man is not responsible for an action unless he could have done otherwise if he had chosen to do otherwise or if his character and desires had been different. This view is obviously correct; in fact, it is essentially a restatement of Aristotle's position. But it is compatible with determinism, for it insists only that the causes of an action must be internal, not that the action must be uncaused. As far as this view is concerned, a man's choice may be determined by his own beliefs, character, and desires (which, in turn, may be determined by previous causes), and yet be free and responsible.

Many philosophers and theologians have thought, however, that this view is not satisfactory and that a man is not responsible for an action unless he not only could have done otherwise *if he had chosen* but also *could have chosen* otherwise. Moreover, they argue, he could have chosen otherwise only if his choice was not simply the result of previous causes such as his beliefs, character, desires, heredity, and environment. In other words, they contend that moral responsibility is incompatible with determinism as it is usually conceived, and that "freedom of a contra-causal kind" is among the conditions of moral responsibility. This was Kant's view, and it has recently been forcefully defended by C. A. Campbell, from whom the words just quoted were taken, and R. M. Chisholm.

On the other side, some determinists have maintained not only that determinism is compatible with moral responsibility, but that moral responsibility presupposes determinism, and that it is really indeterminism that is incompatible with morality.

FREE WILL AND RESPONSIBILITY

It is in this way that the problem of free will and determinism comes up in ethics. Here determinism is the view that every event, including human choices and volitions, is caused by other events and happens as an effect or result of these other events. Indeterminism denies this, and adds that some events, among them human choices and volitions, happen without any cause or explanation. Part of the problem is whether either of these views is true; however, this question belongs to metaphysics and must be left to one side. We can only briefly consider the other part of the problem, namely, whether determinism and indeterminism are incompatible with moral responsibility. The question is not whether X's being free in doing Y is a condition of its being right, wrong, or obligatory. One does not, when he is trying to decide what he ought to do, look to see whether or not he is free. He assumes he is. The question is only whether X's being responsible for Y presupposes his having been free (and if so, free in what sense) in doing Y. But then, according to what was said about the second usage of "responsibility" a little while ago, we are really asking whether it is right to hold X responsible for Y, to praise or blame him and possibly to reward or punish him, if determinism is true or if indeterminism is true. We are asking a question of normative ethics, not, as is usually thought, one of logic or meta-ethics. The question, "Is moral responsibility compatible with determinism (or indeterminism)?" asks not whether determinism (or indeterminism) is *logically* compatible with responsibility, blame, etc., but whether it is *morally* compatible with them. It asks whether we are morally justified in ascribing responsibility, in blaming, etc., if we take determinism (or indeterminism) to be true.

Now, although philosophers differ about this, ascribing responsibility, blaming, punishing, and the like, may be regarded as acts we may or may not perform. We say, for instance, "What you did was wrong, but I don't blame you for doing it." But, if they are acts, then the answer to the question whether it is right to perform them if determinism or if indeterminism is true depends on one's general normative theory of obligation, that is, on one's answer to the question of Chapters 2 and 3. Thus, the determinists who have held that determinism is compatible with moral responsibility have, in their arguments to show this, generally presupposed a teleological theory of obligation, usually a utilitarian one. They argue that it is right to hold people responsible, praise them, punish them, and the like, if and only if doing so makes for the greatest balance of good over evil. In other words, like all other actions, such acts as ascribing responsibility, blaming, and punishing are justified by their results, not by anything in the past. If this view is correct, ascribing responsibility, blaming, and punishing may be justified even if determinism is true (some would add only if determinism is true), for it will not matter that the agent being blamed was not free in the contra-causal sense. All that matters is whether praising or blaming him will or will not have certain results.

Deontologists have sometimes been determinists or held moral responsibility to be consistent with determinism, for example Ross. However, most deontologists have denied that morality is compatible with determinism. They deny that ascribing responsibility, praising, blaming, and punishing are made right or wrong wholly by their results, and they insist that it matters whether the agent in question was contra-causally free or not. For, if he was not, then it is wrong to praise or blame him or even to hold him responsible, while, if he was contra-causally free, it is right not only to hold him responsible, but to praise or blame or otherwise punish or reward him. It may even be obligatory to do so. In short, as only a deontologist can do, they take a retributivist rather than a consequentialist view of the justification of such acts as praising, blaming, and punishing, and they infer that determinism is not consistent with morality and its sanctions.

How one answers the question of the bearing of determinism and indeterminism on ethics depends, then, on one's view about how such acts as praising, blaming, and holding responsible are to be justified morally; this in turn depends on one's basic principles of right and wrong. Earlier I proposed as the most adequate normative theory of obligation a form of mixed deontological theory in which the basic principles are those of beneficence and equality of treatment (distributive justice). This theory is compatible with a retributivist view about responsibility and desert, although such a view would require us to add a third principle to the effect that it is at least prima facie right or obligatory as such to apply sanctions to those who have done wrong and to praise or reward certain sorts of right-doing. But, like Socrates and many others, I find such a retributivist theory of the justification of punishment and other sanctions (or retributive justice) quite incredible. It seems to me they are to be justified, if at all, by their educative, reformatory, preventive, or encouraging effects. This view is compatible with the form of deontologism proposed earlier. For according to our theory, as well as on teleological theories, it is possible to hold that the function of holding people responsible and applying sanctions is not retribution but education, reformation, prevention, and encouragement. All we need to add to what the utilitarians say is that their function is to promote equality as well as welfare.

If we take this consequentialist position about the justification of sanctions and ascriptions of responsibility, then, like the teleologists, we can go on to maintain that they may be justified even if there is no such thing as contra-causal freedom. All that is necessary to justify them is that they actually have a capacity and a tendency to have the desired effects on people's future behavior. In short, according to our theory, we may also conclude that determinism is compatible with moral responsibility, as most recent English-speaking moral philosophers have thought.

However, if we accept such a view of the justification of the use of responsibility-ascriptions and moral sanctions, we must make two assumptions. (1) We must assume that people are normally free to do as they choose. If, by nature, they were like ants, bees, or even monkeys, if they had all been thoroughly brainwashed, if they were all neurotically or psychotically compulsive throughout, or if they were all always under a constant dire threat from a totalitarian ruler of the worst kind, then it would be pointless to try to influence their behavior in the ways that are characteristic of morality (it must be remembered that the threat of punishment is a legal rather than a moral instrument, except in the form of blame and the like). Moral sanctions, internal or external, could not then be expected to have the desired effects. (2) We must also assume that the choices and actions of people normally have reasons and are reasonably predictable, and are not the result of such wholly chance swervings as were attributed to the atoms by the Epicureans or as are now attributed to sub-atomic particles by some indeterminists who appeal to recent physics in support of their position. Otherwise, again, we should have to regard it as generally pointless to try to influence people by such methods as are part of the moral institution of life—holding them responsible, blaming or praising them, inculcating a sense of duty in them, setting them examples, reasoning with them, and so on.

The second assumption is clearly compatible with determinism. The only question is about the first. But a determinist can perfectly well allow that we are often or even normally free to do as we choose, at least if we live in a society that permits us such freedom. That is, he can consistently hold that we are or at least may be free to act and to choose in accordance with our own desires, beliefs, and character. All he is required to insist on is that our beliefs, desires, and traits of character have causes.

It is, however, often argued that the second assumption is incompatible with indeterminism, and that the moral institution of life is therefore inconceivable without determinism. This contention is not entirely convincing. (1) Even if there is some indeterminism in the human sphere, it may still be possible that there are statistical regularities in human behavior of such a sort that our actions are to some extent predictable and influenceable by such things as moral sanctions. I must confess, however, to a feeling that indeterminism makes things rather too "chancy"; it seems to mean that there is an element of sheer chance in our decisions and this hardly seems to be compatible with our being free to do *as we choose.* (2) There may be a third alternative besides determinism and indeterminism. Some of those who believe that morality presupposes contra-causal freedom reject both of these opposing theories, for example, Kant, Campbell, and Chisholm. They deny both that our choices are always caused by previous events in accordance with natural laws and also that they are in any way matters of mere chance. Instead, they argue for a special kind of agency; they hold that a self or person is a unique agent capable of a kind of "self-determination" that is not a function of previous causes and yet is not a matter of chance but of choice, intent, and purpose. Such a view could accept both of the above assumptions, yet reject determinism.

Thus, it is possible to make the two assumptions which are necessary for moral responsibility and not to be a determinist. However, for the reason indicated, I doubt that indeterminism can be regarded as wholly satisfactory. As for the self-determination theory just described, it has not yet, in my opinion, been worked out in any satisfactory way,[7] and a discussion of it would involve us in metaphysical questions we cannot consider here. For this reason, it seems best to try to defend the view that determinism is compatible with moral responsibility, and I have elected to do so, although in doing so I do not mean to imply that I regard determinism as true or that self-determinism is false.

There is still another alternative. This is to argue, first, that determinism is true, and second, that it is inconsistent with moral responsibility and possibly with the whole institution of morality. This view has at least been approximated recently by Paul Edwards and John Hospers and by some interpreters of psychoanalysis. If one adopts this position, however, one must be prepared to propose either that the moral institution of life be radically reconstructed or that it be dropped altogether and replaced by something entirely different. Some such drastic proposal may turn out to be correct, but until its two premises have been more conclusively established than they have been, it seems the better part of valor to espouse the position here taken.

It should be pointed out in this connection that determinism does not entail fatalism, the view that what we do is wholly controlled by something independent of our choices and desires. That determinism does entail fatalism is often assumed by its opponents, and sometimes by its proponents, as it is in the following limerick:

7 But see R. M. Chisholm, *Human Freedom and the Self* (Lawrence: The University Press of Kansas, 1964). Reprinted in Frankena and Granrose, Chap. IV.

There was a young man who said, "Damn!
It grieves me to think that I am
Predestined to move
In a circumscribed groove,
In fact, not a bus, but a tram."

As we saw, however, a determinist may allow that we are normally free to do as we choose, to act in accordance with our own beliefs, desires, and character. Thus, although he may be a fatalist, he need not be one. He may quite consistently regard us more as buses than as trams and more as drivers than as buses. Fatalism does appear to be inconsistent with moral responsibility, but this does not show that determinism is.

It is crucial for our view to hold that in any society with enough social freedom to have a morality, normal human beings are or at least may be free to do as they choose in the sense indicated; we must also hold that our having this sort of freedom is sufficient for the purposes of morality, so that contra-causal freedom is not required. For, if either of these propositions can be shown to be false, it is vain to contend that morality in the form in which we have known it historically is consistent with a non-fatalistic determinism. The first proposition, however, we may regard as plausible enough for present purposes. The only serious doubt that might be cast on it is due to the work of the psychoanalysts and, if I understand them, even they hold that we may be free in the sense in question, at least after we have been successfully psychoanalyzed. The second proposition is harder to be sure about, and much of the debate centers around it. I do not see, however, that it has been shown that morality requires us to be free in a contra-causal sense in addition to being free in the ordinary sense of being free to do as one chooses, free to do Y if one chooses, and free not to do Y if one chooses not to. That the latter is the ordinary sense of "free" is shown by the fact that when I ask you, outside of a philosophical discussion, if you are free or did something freely, you do not look about to see if your decisions are uncaused, but only to see if anything is compelling you or if your actions are an expression of your own desires and character in the light of your own beliefs. So far as I can see, it is morally justifiable to hold people responsible, and to praise and blame them if and insofar as they act freely in this sense, provided, of course, that doing so is in accordance with the principles of beneficence and justice.

On this subject, however, as on most others in our province, one must be careful not to be dogmatic. Milton says that after their fall from heaven some of the devils

reasoned high
Of Providence, Foreknowledge, Will and Fate,
Fixt Fate, free will, foreknowledge absolute,
And found no end, in wandering mazes lost.

Their problem was complicated by certain theological questions we have not raised, but it is always possible that we are as lost as they—possible, but not necessary, for, if earth has any advantage over hell, we can still hope to find an "end," even if we have not already found one.

CHAPTER FIVE

Intrinsic Value and the Good Life

PRELIMINARY REMARKS

Francis Bacon began *Of the Colours of Good and Evil* with the sentence, "In deliberatives the point is, what is good and what is evil, and of good what is greater, and of evil what is the less." If we understand "good" and "evil" to be used here in a nonmoral sense, we too may use this sentence to introduce our present subject. So far the normative questions we have been asking have been strictly ethical or moral: what is morally right, wrong, or obligatory; what is morally good or bad; when are we morally responsible? Now we come to another kind of normative question, one that is not as such ethical or moral but is relevant to ethics and morality, as we saw in Chapter 3. This question, which again we can try to answer only in general outline, may be put in a variety of ways: what is desirable, good, or worthwhile in life? what is the good life as distinct from the morally good life? what values should we pursue for ourselves and others?

The present question, and the normative theory of nonmoral value that seeks to answer it, are relevant to moral philosophy because we cannot or should not determine what is morally right or wrong without considering whether what we do or propose to do will have good or evil results, even though we cannot determine this simply by balancing the quantity of good achieved against the evil. Otherwise, they would not belong to moral philosophy. However, even if they did not belong to moral philosophy, they would be important for one's general philosophy of life. For, even if one is a pure prudentialist, his "deliberatives" will still center on the questions "What is good and what is evil, and of good what is greater, and of evil what is the less?"

Nonmoral evaluations or value judgments may be *particular* like "That is a good car," "Wasn't that a good concert," or "It was good to see you"; or *general* like "Knowledge is good," "All that glitters is not gold," or "It is good for me to draw near to God." A particular value judgment, however, is always implicitly general; when one says that X is good, one must be prepared to say that anything just like it is good and good in the same degree. Also, one must be prepared to give reasons why it is good, and this can only be done in the light of more general value judgments about what is good or at least prima facie good. For example, if one is asked why that was a good concert, one must say something like, "Because it was profoundly moving," which implies that being profoundly moving is a good-making characteristic, at least from an aesthetic point of view. In fact, all evaluations properly so-called are at least implicitly made by reference to some standard or to some set of general judgments about what is good-making or prima facie good. They are not simply expressions of desire or emotion, though they may be occasioned by an emotion or a desire. More will be said about this in the next chapter, however. Just now the point is that what we are looking for in this chapter is the standard or general judgments by which we should make our evaluations.

"GOOD" AND ITS SENSES

It will be convenient to conduct our discussion in terms of the question of what is good, letting it be understood that corresponding things may be said about what is bad, desirable, and so on. Even the term "good" has somewhat different uses that must not be confused. It occurs as a substantive in sentences like, "The good is pleasure" and "Withhold not good from them to whom it is due," but it also has two adjectival uses illustrated by "a good concert" and "Knowledge is good." We must be careful not to confuse "the good" or "the things that are good" with goodness or the property of being good. The terms "value" and "values" are troublesome partly because, as often used, they cover up this distinction, as well as the distinction between being good and being thought good.

However, since "the good" is equivalent to "that to which the adjective good applies," we may take the adjective as central for our discussion. The *Oxford English Dictionary* says, among other things, that "good" is:

> The most general adjective of commendation, implying the existence in a high, or at least satisfactory, degree of characteristic qualities which are either admirable in themselves, or useful for some purpose.

This elucidation points out that saying something is good is not quite prescribing that we do it or saying that we ought to bring it into existence, but rather commending it, with the implication that one is doing so on certain grounds, that is, because of certain facts about it. Whether this view is entirely adequate may be left to the next chapter. What is relevant now is that one may commend a thing or say it is good on various grounds. If the thing is a person, motive, intention, deed, or trait of character, one may commend it on moral grounds; then, one is using "good" in the moral sense basic to the previous chapter, but not under discussion here. One may also commend something on nonmoral grounds, and then one may apply the term "good" to all sorts of things, not just to persons and their acts or dispositions. These nonmoral grounds, moreover, are themselves various, yielding a number of different senses or uses of "good," the main ones of which we must now distinguish. (Perhaps one should call them different "uses" rather than "senses" of "good," since presumably "good" always has the same *meaning*—roughly that given by the *Oxford English Dictionary*—and is only being applied on different *grounds* or from different *points of view.*)

1. One may say, pointing to a stick, "That would make a good lever." Then, one is saying it is good simply on the ground of its *usefulness* for the purpose at hand, whether this purpose is a good one or not.

2. One may also say that something is good on the ground that it is a *means,* necessary, sufficient, or both, to a good end, as when one says, "It is a good idea to go to the dentist twice a year." Then it is *extrinsically* or *instrumentally* good, or good *as a means.* Except for the miser, money and material goods (not counting works of art or things of natural beauty) are good only in this sense.

3. Works of art and things of natural beauty may also be said to be good on the ground that one who looks at them normally has a good or rewarding experience. Then, we may say that they have *inherent* goodness.

4. However, not all goodness is extrinsic or even inherent in these ways. We also sometimes say that things are good, desirable, or worthwhile *in themselves, as ends, intrinsically.* When someone asks, "What is ________ good for?" the answer may be given by trying to exhibit its usefulness, extrinsic value, or inherent goodness; but one may also try to show (and here the final appeal must be "Try it and see") that it is enjoyable or otherwise good in itself. Thus A. E. Housman in *The Pursuit of Knowledge* decries the effort to defend learning on utilitarian or moral grounds, though he admits it does have uses and extrinsic values, and seeks to justify it by its own worth alone. In fact, it is hard to see how money, cars, and other material possessions, even paintings, can have any goodness or value at all,

extrinsic or inherent, if the experiences they make possible are not in some way enjoyable or good in themselves.

5. Earlier I contrasted the morally good life and the good life in the nonmoral sense (e.g., the happy life). In view of what was just said, we may call the latter the intrinsically good life. Then we can also say of certain sorts of experience that they are good because they contribute to the good life, or because if they are included in one's life they make it intrinsically better. One might call such *contributively good* experiences *means* to the good life, but it is better to think of them as *parts* of it. Mill does this when he says that money and knowledge are both originally sought as means to happiness but may come to be sought for their own sakes, as in the case of a miser or a scientist, when they become parts of happiness.

The following table will summarize this account of the uses of "good."

I. Moral values = things that are good on moral grounds.
II. Nonmoral values.
  A. Utility values = things that are good because of their usefulness for some purpose.
  B. Extrinsic values = things that are good because they are means to what is good.
  C. Inherent values = things that are good because the experience of contemplating them is good or rewarding in itself.
  D. Intrinsic values = things that are good in themselves or good because of their own intrinsic properties.
  E. Contributory values = things that are good because they contribute to the intrinsically good life or are parts of it.
  F. Final values = things that are good on the whole (to be explained in a moment).

It should be observed that the same thing can be good in more than one sense, as is knowledge. In fact, Dewey sought to break down the distinction between what is good as a means and what is good as an end, partly because he realized that most of the things we do or live through are both good or bad in themselves and good or bad in their results. His premise was correct but his conclusion need not be drawn. All that follows is that we must constantly look for both kinds of values in our activities, instead of thinking that some are good only as means and others only as ends. We must also notice that the same thing can be good in one sense and bad in another. Going to a dentist is good as a means but bad in itself, though in totaling up the scores we must remember Dewey's point. An action or experience may even be intrinsically good, and morally bad or wrong, or vice versa, as we shall see.

It follows that we must be careful if someone says "X is good" or asks "Is X good?" We know, of course, that he is commending X or asking if it should be commended and favored; but, before we can agree or answer, we must try to ascertain on what ground he is saying X is good or from what point of view he is asking if it is good. Of course, he may be saying that it is good on the whole or from all points of view, or he may be asking if it is good in this sense. But we must find this out. We find out, of course, by discovering what reasons he gives or is willing to listen to for his judgment. In fact, if someone uses the word "good" in an unqualified way, as we usually do (i.e., we do not usually put in qualifiers like "morally," "extrinsically," etc.), we probably must first take it to mean good on the whole, unless the context makes clear that it does not mean this. We must then wait for the discussion to reveal any error on our part. We tend to use the word in a global, inclusive way, and to pin our grounds down only if we have to.

Perhaps too, what we want to achieve, if possible, is usually not just a judgment about a thing's value in some one of these senses but a total evaluation of its value on the whole. This is another part of Dewey's critique of the distinction between extrinsic and intrinsic goodness that is well-taken. But it still remains true that in order to come to a judgment about whether something is good on the whole or good in any of the other senses, we must first determine what its intrinsic value is, what the intrinsic value of its consequences or of the experiences of contemplating it is, or how much it contributes to the intrinsically good life. Our task, therefore, is to determine the criteria or standards of intrinsic goodness and badness. What are the grounds on which things, or rather activities, experiences, and lives may correctly be said to be good, desirable, or worthwhile as ends or in themselves?

THEORIES ABOUT WHAT IS GOOD AS AN END: HEDONISM AND NON-HEDONISM

It goes without saying that there have been many different answers to this question. Plato presents two of them for debate in the *Philebus:* the view that pleasure is the good, the true goal of every living being, and what everyone ought to aim at; and the view that intelligence, knowledge, and wisdom are better and more excellent than pleasure for all who are capable of them. The first of these views is called *hedonism* and has had many proponents from the time of Eudoxus and Epicurus to the present.

What does the hedonistic theory of value maintain? First of all, a hedonist about the good need not be a hedonist about the right. To hold that the right act is that which produces at least as great a balance of pleasure over pain for self or world as any alternative is to hold a hedonistic teleological theory of obligation. One may, however, adopt a hedonistic theory of value without adopting any such theory of obligation. A hedonist about the good may be a deontologist about the right; roughly speaking, Butler, Kant, and Sidgwick combine hedonism about the former with deontologism about the latter.

Secondly, a hedonist about the good says, approximately, that the good is pleasure. But this is apt to be misleading. "Pleasure" is ambiguous. It may mean "experiences that are pleasant" or it may mean the feeling or hedonic tone of "pleasantness" that such experiences have. Now a hedonist about the good is not necessarily *defining* the term "good." He need not say that "good" means "pleasant" or that goodness is pleasantness. He may hold this, but most hedonists have not offered definitions in this sense. A hedonist does, however, offer an equation of a kind: he asserts that the good is pleasure, or that whatever is pleasant is good and vice versa.

Even this statement is inaccurate, however, and to see just what a hedonist about the good is claiming we must use a series of statements.

1. Happiness = pleasure, or happiness = pleasantness.
2. All pleasures are intrinsically good, or whatever is pleasant in itself is good in itself. A hedonist may admit that some pleasures are morally bad or wrong, or that some are bad because of their results.
3. Only pleasures are intrinsically good, or whatever is good in itself is pleasant in itself. A hedonist may allow other things, even pains, to be good as means or even morally good or right.
4. Pleasantness is the criterion of intrinsic goodness. It is what makes things good as ends. It is not just a coincidence that what is pleasant is good in itself and vice versa.

All hedonists about the good accept these four propositions. Beyond this point they may differ, however. They usually hold that pleasures differ in kind or quality, for example that mental pleasures are different from physical ones. But Epicurus and Bentham hold that such differences in quality make no difference to their goodness or value. As the latter puts it, "Quantity of pleasure being equal, pushpin is as good as poetry." Non-hedonists were shocked at this, but so was Mill. Mill maintained, therefore, that differences in quality of pleasure entail differences in value—that mental pleasures are or may be better than physical ones just because of the *kind* of pleasure involved, whether they contain a greater *quantity* of pleasure or not. Thus we must add a fifth statement, which some hedonists accept and others reject:

5. The intrinsic goodness of an activity or experience is proportional to the quantity of pleasure it contains (or rather to the quantitative balance of pleasure over pain contained in it or intrinsic to it).

Quantitative hedonists accept (5); *qualitative* hedonists deny it. Critics of hedonism often say that Mill's denying it is inconsistent with his being a hedonist, but this is only because they identify hedonism with quantitative hedonism. Where Mill gets into difficulty is in trying to formulate the principle of utility in non-quantitative terms, a point we made in Chapter 3.

As against this, *non-hedonists* may hold that pleasure is *a* good, but they must all deny that pleasure is *the* good—they may allow that pleasantness is a good-making characteristic, but they must insist that it is not the only one. More accurately, in terms of the above propositions, they may admit (1) and (2) and even (3), but must reject (4) and (5). Usually, however, they reject (1), (2), and (3) as well. As to what is good as an end or good-making, besides or instead of pleasure, or what the criterion of intrinsic value is, they may and do take a variety of positions, some of which we shall indicate as we go along.

THE FIRST LINE OF DEBATE

Two main kinds of argument have been used in the debate between the hedonists and the non-hedonists. First, there is a psychological line of argument. Hedonists, quantitative or qualitative, have usually argued that pleasure is the good in itself because it is what we all, ultimately at least, desire or aim at. Thus Aristotle reports Eudoxus as maintaining pleasure to be the good because he saw all things aiming at it. Epicurus used the same argument. And Mill writes that

> . . . if human nature is so constituted as to desire nothing which is not either a part of happiness [pleasure] or a means of happiness, we can have no other proof, and we require no other, that these are the only things desirable.[1]

He then argues that human nature is so constituted and concludes that pleasure and pleasure alone is good as an end, basically at least.

The premise of this argument is a psychological doctrine, a theory of human nature, which is called *psychological hedonism.* The conclusion, however, is a value judgment. As a result, many non-hedonists, from G. E. Moore on, have attacked the argument as illogical. From

(a) Pleasure and pleasure alone is desired as an end,

they say one cannot correctly infer:

(c) ∴ Pleasure and pleasure alone is good as an end.

They are right, of course, since (c) contains terms which are not present in (a). But Mill explicitly states that he does not regard his argument as a *logical* proof, and Eudoxus and Epicurus might well agree with him. Hence, the criticisms of Moore and his followers are beside the point. Mill's contention is not that (c) follows logically from (a) but that (a) is true as a theory of human nature; and that, if human nature is so constituted as always to aim at pleasure, then it is absurd or unreasonable to deny that pleasure is the good, even though it is logically possible.

[1] *Utilitarianism,* near end of Chap. 4. See selections in Frankena and Granrose, Chap. V.

Thus interpreted, the argument seems to me a potent one, if (a) can be shown to be true. In any case, however, it is easy enough for a hedonist to put his argument in a form that is entirely valid:

(a) Pleasure and pleasure alone is desired as an end.
(b) What is desired as an end and only what is desired as an end is good as an end.
(c) ∴ Pleasure and pleasure alone is good as an end.

Then the only way to attack it is to throw doubt on either (a) or (b).

Many non-hedonists accept (b) and reject (a). Aristotle, for example, says that to claim that the end at which all things aim is not necessarily good is to talk nonsense; in fact, he begins by arguing that the good may be defined as that at which all things aim. He agrees that all things aim at happiness but denies that happiness is pleasure. Happiness is excellent activity of the soul, he contends; and for him this means activity in accordance with the moral and especially the intellectual virtues or excellences, the latter including science, wisdom, and other forms of knowledge. This excellence of activity, he says, is what we seek as our end, not pleasure. Pleasure is an accompaniment of the achieving and exercising of these excellences. It is not the object of our desires, it is the felt satisfaction we get when we achieve what we desire. This argument is very similar to that of Butler against psychological egoism, which is no accident since such egoism and psychological hedonism usually go together. The claim is that the psychological hedonist is putting the cart before the horse. We do not desire knowledge and the other excellences because they give pleasure; we obtain pleasure from them because we desire them and they satisfy our desires.

This argument has a good deal of force, though we must remember John Clarke's countermove, described in Chapter 2. The argument does not prove that hedonism is mistaken as a theory of value, even if we accept (b), but it seems to me to show that psychological hedonism has not been proved, may not be true, and cannot be used as part of an argument to establish a hedonistic theory of value. If Clarke's rejoinder does not hold up, it even shows psychological hedonism of the kind in question to be false. In any case, it is very doubtful that we desire things in proportion to the amount of pleasure or satisfaction we expect from them. Another point should be mentioned as helping to throw doubt on psychological hedonism. Non-hedonists often point out, again correctly, that if we consciously take pleasure as our end, we somehow miss it, while if we pursue and attain other things for their own sakes, not calculating the pleasure they will bring, we somehow gain pleasure. This is known as "the hedonistic paradox."

Other non-hedonists follow Aristotle in accepting (b) and rejecting (a) and (c), but differ with him about what the good is. Where he stressed the intellectual excellences, the Stoics emphasized the moral ones. Augustine and Aquinas follow the same general line of argument but finally identify the good with God or with communion with God. Nietzsche identifies the good with power, contending that this is what we all aim at, although by power he does not mean merely the sort of thing Napoleon had, but all kinds of excellence of the human spirit; Nietzsche believed that Leonardo da Vinci had power in this sense. The Hegelian idealists like F. H. Bradley also hold that the good is what we all seek; however, they claim, much as Nietzsche does although in a less radical spirit, that the good we seek is self-realization.

THE SECOND LINE OF DEBATE

All of these writers agree that what we aim at is the good; and they then argue that human nature is so constituted that we all aim at X (pleasure, excellence, God, power, self-realization), concluding that X is the good or the criterion of what is good as an end. We cannot possibly discuss their rather speculative theories here, for such a discussion would require a good deal of psychology and some metaphysics. We shall have to rest our position on the second kind of argument used in the debates between hedonists and non-hedonists. It is interesting to note, however, that on the basis of the first kind of argument, two general sorts of things have been claimed to be good as ends: on the one hand, something like pleasure, enjoyment, or satisfaction; on the other, some form of excellence or self-perfection. The term "happiness" has been used for both. We shall return to this point later.

Many writers, some hedonists like Sidgwick and some non-hedonists like Plato, Moore, and Ross, reject the above kind of argument on the general ground that a thing is not good because, or if and only if, it is desired. Instead, these writers appeal to a kind of reflective review of the sorts of things we seem to take as ends or as good in themselves to see which ones hold up under inspection and whether one can discover any criteria by which they may be evaluated. Sidgwick, Moore, and Ross think of this inspection as a process of intuition of self-evident judgments, but it is not necessary to do so, and it is not clear that Plato did. The main point is that the review must be reflective and must limit itself rigorously to the question of what is good in itself or apart from its consequences and moral implications, the question being roughly, "What sorts of things is it rational to desire for their own sakes?"

In their reviews such writers consider some or all of the following candidates, sometimes dividing them into categories like "biological," "physical," "mental," "social," and "spiritual":

Life, consciousness, and activity
Health and strength
Pleasures and satisfactions of all or certain kinds
Happiness, beatitude, contentment, etc.

Truth
Knowledge and true opinion of various kinds, understanding, wisdom
Beauty, harmony, proportion in objects contemplated
Aesthetic experience
Morally good dispositions or virtues
Mutual affection, love, friendship, cooperation
Just distribution of goods and evils
Harmony and proportion in one's own life
Power and experiences of achievement
Self-expression
Freedom
Peace, security
Adventure and novelty
Good reputation, honor, esteem, etc.

Religious experiences or values, which many rate highest among intrinsic goods, are not mentioned separately in this list because they presuppose the existence of God and so raise questions that cannot be dealt with here. The communion with and love or knowledge of God that Augustine and Aquinas regard as the highest good would, however, presumably come under our headings of knowledge and mutual love. Other intrinsically good religious experiences would also probably fall under these or other headings.

Of course, the items listed overlap and others could be added. Reviewing such a list, philosophers have come out with various smaller tables of intrinsic goods or values. The triad of truth, goodness, and beauty, usually spelled with capital letters, is a classic one. Nicolai Hartmann includes all of the things mentioned. Moore emphasizes certain pleasures, beauty, aesthetic experience, knowledge, and personal affections. Ross's list is much the same, but it omits beauty and includes the moral virtues and the just apportionment of happiness to desert. He ranks virtue above knowledge and knowledge above pleasure. Plato, in the *Philebus,* argues that the good life is a "mixed life," containing the following ingredients, which he ranks in the order given:

a. Measure, moderation, fitness, etc.
b. Proportion, beauty, perfection, etc.
c. Mind and wisdom
d. Sciences, arts, and true opinion
e. Pure or painless pleasures of the soul itself.

All of the men just mentioned are non-hedonists. Of the five hedonistic theses listed earlier, they all deny (4) and (5). Most of them deny (2), insisting that some pleasures are intrinsically bad, for example, pleasures gained by treachery, or those involving a morally bad disposition like cruelty or malice or the enjoyment of what is evil or ugly. Some would also reject (3), arguing that there are some intrinsically good things that do not contain pleasure, though they may cause or occasion it, for example, beauty, truth, and virtue. Plato, like Aristotle, would reject (1) as well. Sidgwick, on the other hand, is a hedonist. He argues, in his review of proposed goods, first, that nothing is good in itself except desirable experiences or states of consciousness, and second, that experiences or states of consciousness are desirable in themselves only if and insofar as they contain pleasure. That is, he is a quantitative hedonist and accepts all five of the hedonist theses; for him pleasantness, or more accurately, balance of pleasure over pain, is the criterion or standard of nonmoral value.

SOME CONCLUSIONS Reflecting on the longer list of proposed intrinsic values myself, I come to the following conclusions. It seems to me that all of them may be kept on the list, and perhaps others may be added, if it is understood that it is the *experience* of them that is good in itself. Sidgwick seems to me to be right on this point. Take the traditional triad, for instance. It seems to me that truth is not itself intrinsically good. It may not even be known. What is good in itself is knowledge of or belief in the truth. The same point may be applied to beauty, harmony, proportion, or the just distribution of goods and evils (the consideration of the last item bears on the validity of utilitarianism, as we saw in Chapter 3). These are not themselves intrinsically valuable; what is intrinsically good is the contemplation or experiencing of them. In themselves, they are inherent rather than intrinsic goods. As for virtue—as Aristotle said, we can be virtuous while asleep, when nothing of intrinsic value is going on. The experience of acting virtuously and of feeling morally good emotions, however, may be intrinsically good as far as it goes. I shall argue that it is.

We must, I think, distinguish between pleasure and happiness. "Pleasure" suggests rather specific feelings, whereas "happiness" does not. We can speak of "pleasures" but hardly of "happinesses." "Pleasure" also suggests physical or "lower" pleasures more than "happiness" does. Again, it suggests short-run and superficial enjoyment rather than the longer span and more profound satisfaction connoted by "happiness." Finally, phrases like "the pleasant life" and "a life of pleasure" call to mind something rather different from the phrase "the happy life." In fact, in ordinary discourse, we must and do distinguish a whole family of kinds of satisfactoriness that experiences and lives may have. Pleasantness is only one of them. Happiness, contentment, and beatitude are others. In this sense, the hedonist's thesis (1) is a mistake, though he is right in thinking that happiness is a kind of satisfactoriness. He could, of course, redefine the terms "pleasure" and "pleasant" to cover all of these good-making qualities of experience, but doing this is like trying to redefine the word "red" to cover all of the colors.

Hedonists are right, I think, in holding their thesis (2), namely, that every pleasure or enjoyment is, taken as such and by itself, intrinsically good. Against this, as we have seen, non-hedonists usually argue that there are bad pleasures—pleasures that are bad, not only because of their consequences, but in themselves. But, so far as I can see, the non-hedonists never really show this. I agree that malicious pleasure and the enjoyment of cruelty and ugliness, if they really occur, are bad, but are they bad *qua* pleasures or enjoyments? They may be *morally* bad in themselves or bad because they are symptoms of some defect or derangement of personality, but their being bad in such senses must not be confused with their being bad *qua* pleasures or enjoyments. Non-hedonists never make clear that they are not confusing these kinds of badness. I am still inclined to think, therefore, that every pleasure has some intrinsic goodness, although, of course, an experience that is pleasant may also have bad-making features that make its *total* score negative, e.g., a malicious pleasure.

What about hedonist thesis (3): that nothing is intrinsically good if it does not contain pleasure? If, as I suggested, we distinguish other kinds of satisfactoriness besides pleasure, then thesis (3) is not quite true. But the broader and somewhat similar thesis that nothing is intrinsically good unless it contains some kind of satisfactoriness seems to me to be clearly true. Thus, I think that knowledge, excellence, power, and so on, are simply cold, bare, and valueless in themselves unless they are experienced with some kind of enjoyment or satisfaction.

If we distinguish kinds of satisfactoriness, as we have, then the thesis of the quantitative hedonists [i.e., hedonist thesis (5)] must be rejected. For then, intrinsic value cannot be proportional to quantity of pleasure or to balance of pleasure over pain. Nor can we restate the thesis to say that intrinsic value is proportional to quantity of satisfactoriness or balance of satisfactoriness over unsatisfactoriness, for satisfactorinesses, for example, beatitude and contentment, differ in kind and hence are incommensurable. There is this much truth, at least, in Mill's doctrine that quality affects value. It follows, of course, that a calculus of intrinsic value in purely quantitative terms is not possible, as was hinted in Chapter 3.

Again, if we distinguish kinds of satisfactoriness besides pleasure, then pleasantness cannot be *the* criterion of intrinsic goodness or the only good-making feature of experiences, and hedonist thesis (4) is false. In reply one might contend, however, that there are no good-making qualities of experience except the different kinds of satisfactoriness mentioned and other kinds if there are any. Then one would still be a quasi-hedonist; the standard of evaluation would not be pleasure but it would be a set of related kinds of satisfactoriness. I am not sure this contention is mistaken, but I doubt it is true. Some non-hedonists like Plato, Aristotle, Moore, Ross, and C. D. Broad argue that there are other good-making features of experiences besides pleasantness, happiness, etc., other factors that also may contribute to the intrinsic value of experiences. For example, they maintain that harmony and knowledge are such features. They contend that just as the presence of pleasure makes an experience so far good, so does the presence of harmony or of knowledge or understanding make it so far good. And if an experience contains both some kind of satisfactoriness and harmony or knowledge, then it is, or at least may be, intrinsically better than it would be if it contained only that kind of satisfactoriness, even if the amount of satisfactoriness involved were the same. This kind of argument is not conclusive, but it is plausible; at this point it is very difficult to be certain what one must say. If the argument is correct, then hedonist thesis (4) is false even in its quasi-hedonist form.

In fact, I am inclined to think the non-hedonists are right—that there is something else besides enjoyableness or satisfactoriness that makes activities and experiences good in themselves, and I suggest that this is always the presence of some kind or degree of excellence. Many of our activities and experiences involve or are involved in an endeavor to achieve excellence by some standard appropriate to them, for example, athletic activities, artistic creation, and science or history. It seems to me that what makes gymnastics, knowledge, and aesthetic creation good in themselves is not just the amount of enjoyment they provide but also the fact that they involve the exercise of an ability or skill or the attainment of some degree of excellence by some standard, and that the same thing is true of many other kinds of activity and experience, though the activities and standards involved may be of very different kinds, aesthetic (beauty), intellectual (truth), athletic (bodily skill), moral (rightness and moral goodness), and so on.

Thus, when I scrutinize the items on our list and exclude those that pertain to what I shall call the form or pattern of the good life, it seems to me that they are made good by the presence in them of one or both of two factors: pleasure or satisfaction and some kind of excellence. Similarly, I would say that what is bad in itself is so because of the presence either of pain or unhappiness or of some kind of defect or lack of excellence. It may be, then, that an enjoyable experience is made bad by the presence of some defect that cancels out the goodness due to its enjoyableness; the case of a malicious pleasure, which involves a moral defect, may be an example.

Although I am ready to agree with the non-hedonist to this extent, I still think that an experience or activity is not good in itself unless it is pleasant or satisfactory, or, in other words, that some kind of satisfactoriness is a necessary condition of something's being intrinsically good. It also seems to me that being enjoyable is a sufficient condition of something's being good, at least when it is not cancelled out by the presence of some defect, for example, the experience of enjoying a sharp cheese. To this extent I am ready to go with the quasi-hedonist. How does excellence come into the picture then? I would answer that it does so by making experiences or activities better or worse than they would be otherwise. In other words, I would hold that what is intrinsically satisfying in some way is good in itself and vice versa, but deny that what is good in itself is always good only because it is satisfying, or that it is good in proportion to its satisfactoriness.

THE GOOD LIFE What of the good life, the life it would be rational to choose? If what precedes is correct, the good life will be a "mixed life," as Plato said, consisting of activities and experiences of the kinds listed earlier, that is, of activities and experiences that are enjoyable or both excellent in some degree and enjoyable. We may think of these experiences and activities as making up the *content* of the good life. With his usual insight, however, Plato insisted that the good life must also have *form*. By this he meant *pattern*, and he thought that, for a life to be good, it must be harmonious. We may wish to extend his conception of pattern somewhat, but he was surely right in mentioning it. Any life will willy-nilly have some pattern or other, and it is reasonable to think that some patterns are better than others. D. H. Parker, staying close to Plato, thought that one's life should have such features as unity in variety, balance, rhythm, and hierarchy. A. N. Whitehead, closer to romanticism and evolutionism, thought it should include novelty and adventure, as well as continuity and tradition, and that it should include them in some kind of rhythm of alternation.

There is a view abroad today—ever since the romantic era—which disparages both satisfactoriness and excellence in favor of autonomy, authenticity, commitment, creativity, decision, doing your own thing, freedom, self-expression, striving, struggle, and the like. This view is not tenable in any literal or extreme form, in my opinion, but it contains an important truth, namely, that the best life one is capable of must have form, not just in the sense of pattern, but in the sense of being inspired by a certain attitude, posture, or "life-style." Whitehead called this "subjective form" and thought that reverence should be the dominant style in our lives, though he mentioned others. Autonomy seems to me to come in here, as well as the other things just listed, but I should want to add rationality and related dispositions like objectivity and intellectual responsibility too. And perhaps this is where one should mention love again. At least, if psychologists like Erich Fromm are right, then for one's life to be good, not just in the moral but in the nonmoral sense, one must not be too concerned with the goodness of one's life, but rather with causes and objects outside oneself.

Just what content, pattern, and subjective form the good life has will, no doubt, vary considerably from person to person. To find the answer one must, to a large extent, depend on one's own experience and reflection aided by that of others with experience and wisdom. I doubt that any fixed order or pattern can be laid down for everyone, as Plato and Ross thought. Human nature may be much the same everywhere, and I believe it is, otherwise psychology would be virtually impossible; however, human nature seems to vary too much for any fixed conception of it to be drawn up in detail. Even if all of the items we have mentioned are found to be good, to some extent at least, by everyone, it may and, in fact, seems still to be true that their ranking and arrangement must be somewhat relative. For some people the good life seems to include more peace and security and for others more adventure and novelty, although every life should and does include some of each. If writers like Ruth Benedict are right, the relativity is even more radical than this example suggests; however, even if they go too far, this example at least shows that one must leave a good deal of room for variety in one's conception of the good life, if not in one's list of goods.

We must also remember the point touched on in our discussion of justice—that people's needs and capacities not only differ, but differ in such a way that the good life of one may not be as good intrinsically as that of another. It may be, for example, that A's capacities in an intellectual way are such that the best life of which he is capable simply cannot include much of some of the items mentioned. Then, other things being equal, his best life may be, not only different from, but in itself less good than that of which B is capable. It does not follow, however, that A must be treated as a second-class citizen, as Plato and Aristotle thought. It may still be, as we held earlier, that A is as good as B in the sense that they are, so far as possible, to be treated equally. I firmly believe that the doctrine of the equal intrinsic value of every human being as such is valid, but it is valid only as a principle of what is right or obligatory. It is not valid as a value judgment about the intrinsic worthwhileness of different good lives.

We may connect the discussion of this chapter with what was said before by making two observations. One is that it is to the good life in this sense that morality, like everything else, is or should be a minister. The other is that morality is not to be a minister merely to one's own good life but to that of others as well and, therefore, may restrict one in one's pursuit of what is good—through the principles of beneficence and justice. Virtue, as Socrates says in the *Meno,* is not the power to achieve the good or obtain good things; it is acting justly, honestly, temperately, and, we must add, benevolently.

One thing more. As was indicated, morally right action is one kind of activity that satisfies a standard of excellence, and so being morally right is a kind of excellence and may be one of the factors making an activity intrinsically good—not just good in a moral but in a nonmoral sense. Thus, Alyosha exclaims at one point in *The Brothers Karamazov,* "How good it is to do something good!" Similarly, as in the example of malicious pleasures, an experience may be made bad or at least worse intrinsically by the fact that having it is immoral. If this is so, then for normal human beings one's life may be better or worse in itself because it includes morally right or wrong action. In this sense virtue is its own reward. It is important to remember this when we come to the question of why we should be moral.

CHAPTER SIX

Meaning and Justification

META-ETHICS AND ITS QUESTIONS

Thus far, except for Chapter 1, we have been engaged in normative ethics, although we have also included a good bit of analysis and conceptual clarification, as well as some psychology. In other words, we have been endeavoring to arrive at acceptable principles of obligation and general judgments of value in the light of which to determine what is morally right, wrong, or obligatory, and what or who is morally good, bad, or responsible. As we saw in Chapter 1, however, ethics also includes another kind of inquiry called meta-ethics. Meta-ethics does not propound any moral principles or goals for action, except possibly by implication; as such it consists entirely of philosophical analysis. In fact, recent moral philosophy has concerned itself very largely with meta-ethical analysis; it has been primarily interested in clarification and understanding rather than in normative ethics, though it has included some discussion of punishment, civil disobedience, war, etc., and much debate about utilitarianism. For all that, what it has been doing is most important, since any reflective person should have some understanding of the meaning and justification of his ethical judgments, especially in this age when our general thinking about principles and values is said to be in a state of crisis. In any case, we ourselves must see what sort of justification, if any, can be claimed for the normative positions we have taken.

As usually conceived, meta-ethics asks the following questions. (1) What is the meaning or definition of ethical terms or concepts like "right," "wrong," "good," "bad"? What is the nature, meaning, or function of judgments in which these and similar terms or concepts occur? What are the rules for the use of such terms and sentences? (2) How are moral uses of such terms to be distinguished from nonmoral ones, moral judgments from other normative ones? What is the meaning of "moral" as contrasted with "nonmoral"? (3) What is the analysis or meaning of related terms or concepts like "action," "conscience," "free will," "intention," "promising," "excusing," "motive," "responsibility," "reason," "voluntary"? (4) Can ethical and value judgments be proved, justified, or shown valid? If so, how and in what sense? Or, what is the logic of moral reasoning and of reasoning about value? Of these (1) and (4) are the more standard problems of meta-ethics; but (2) and (3) have been receiving much attention lately. We have touched a little on all of them, but will now concentrate on (1) and (4).

Of these two problems, it is (4) that is primary. What we mainly want to know is whether the moral and value judgments we accept are justified or not; and if so, on what grounds. Question (1) is not in itself important in the same way. Apart from conceptual understanding—which is important to the pure philosopher—we need to be concerned about the meaning or nature of ethical and value judgments only if this helps us to understand whether and how they may be justified, only if it helps us to know which of them are acceptable or valid. I shall therefore state and discuss the main answers to question (1) if and when they are relevant to the discussion of question (4). It is not easy to classify all of the different theories of the meaning of ethical and value terms and judgments, but they seem to fall under three general types: *definist* theories, *intuitionism* or *non-naturalism,* and *noncognitive* or *nondescriptivist* theories. I shall explain them as they become relevant.

For the purposes of such discussions as these, moral judgments and nonmoral normative judgments are usually lumped together. This is a risky procedure, for it may be that rather different accounts must be given of the meaning and justification of the two kinds of judgments. Nevertheless, for convenience, we too shall adopt this procedure in our review of the various meta-ethical theories, and use the expression "ethical judgments" to cover all relevant normative and value judgments, not just moral ones.

THEORIES OF JUSTIFICATION

One way of putting question (4) is to ask whether our basic ethical judgments can be justified in any objective way similar to those in which our factual judgments can be justified. It is, therefore, by a natural impulse that many philosophers have sought to show that certain ethical judgments are actually rooted in fact or, as it used to be put, in "the nature of things" as this is revealed either by empirical inquiry, by metaphysical construction, or by divine revelation. How else, they ask, could one possibly hope to justify them as against rival judgments? If our chosen ethical judgments are not based on fact, on the natures and relations of things, then they must be arbitrary and capricious or at best conventional and relative. One who follows this line of thought, however, seems to be committed to claiming that ethical judgments can be derived logically from factual ones, empirical or nonempirical. Opponents have therefore countered by contending that this cannot be done, since one cannot get an Ought out of an Is or a Value out of a Fact.

Now, we do sometimes seem to justify an ethical judgment by an appeal to fact. Thus, we say that a certain act is wrong because it injures someone, or that a certain painting is good because it has symmetry. However, it becomes clear on a moment's thought that our conclusion does not rest on our factual premise alone. In the first case, we are tacitly assuming that injurious acts are wrong, which is a moral principle; and in the second, that paintings with symmetry are good, which is a value judgment. In such cases, then, we are not justifying our original ethical judgment by reference to fact alone but also by reference to a *more basic* ethical premise. The question is whether our *most basic* ethical or value premises can be derived logically from factual ones alone.

This would mean that conclusions with terms like "ought" and "good" in them can be logically inferred from premises, none of which contain these terms; this simply cannot be done by the rules of ordinary inductive or deductive logic. To try to do so is essentially to argue that A is B, ∴ A is C, without introducing any premise connecting B and C. In this sense, those who insist that we cannot go from Is to Ought or from Fact to Value are correct. Such an inference is logically invalid unless there is a special third logic permitting us to do so. It has, in fact, been suggested by some recent writers that there is such a special logic sanctioning certain direct inferences from factual premises to conclusions about what is right or good, that is, an ethical logic with "rules of inference" like "If X is injurious, then X is wrong." But the theory and the rules of such a logic have not yet been satisfactorily worked out, and until they are we can hardly take this possibility seriously. In any case, it is hard to see how such a "rule of inference" differs in substance from the "premise" that injurious acts are wrong, or how its justification will be different.

DEFINIST THEORIES, NATURALISTIC AND METAPHYSICAL

There is, however, one possibility that must be taken seriously. This is the definist view that Ought can be defined in terms of Is, and Value in terms of Fact. For if such definitions are acceptable, then, by virtue of them, one can go logically from Is to Ought or from Fact to Value. For example, if "We ought to do..." means "We are required by society to do...," then from "Society requires that we keep promises," it follows that we ought to keep promises. It will not do to reply, as some have, that no such definitions are possible since we cannot get an Ought out of an Is, for that is to beg the question. We must, therefore, take a closer look at definist theories.

According to such theories ethical terms can be defined in terms of nonethical ones, and ethical sentences can be translated into nonethical ones of a factual kind. For example, R. B. Perry proposes such definitions as these:

"good" means "being an object of favorable interest (desire),"
"right" means "being conducive to harmonious happiness."[1]

For him, then, to say that X is good is simply another way of saying that it is an object of desire, and to say that Y is right is just another way of saying that it is conducive to harmonious happiness. A theologian might claim that "right" means "commanded by God"; according to him, then, saying that Y is right is merely a shorter way of saying that it is commanded by God. On all such views, ethical judgments are disguised assertions of fact of some kind. Those who say, as Perry does, that they are disguised assertions of empirical fact are called *ethical naturalists,* and those who regard them as disguised assertions of metaphysical or theological facts are called *metaphysical moralists.*[2] Many different theories of both kinds are possible, depending on the definitions proposed. In each case, moreover, the definition presented may be advanced as a *reportive* one, simply explicating what we ordinarily mean by the term being defined, or as a *reforming proposal* about what it should be used to mean. Perry's definitions are offered as reforming proposals, since he thinks our ordinary use of "good" and "right" is confused and vague. F. C. Sharp, on the other hand, offers the following as reportive definitions:

"good" means "desired upon reflection,"
"right" means "desired when looked at from an impersonal point of view."[3]

In offering definitions or translations of ethical terms and judgments, a definist also tells us how such judgments are to be justified. For example, when Perry tells us that "good" means "being an object of desire," he also tells us that we can test empirically whether X is good simply by determining whether it is desired or not. In general, on a naturalistic theory, ethical judgments can be justified by empirical inquiry just as ordinary and scientific factual statements can; and on any metaphysical theory, they can be justified

1 *Realms of Value* (Cambridge, Mass.: Harvard University Press, 1954), pp. 3, 107, 109. See selections in Frankena and Granrose, Chap. VI.

2 Most writers today use "naturalism" to cover all kinds of definism.

3 *Ethics* (New York: The Century Co., 1928), pp. 109, 410–11.

by whatever methods one can use to justify metaphysical or theological propositions. Either way they are rooted in the nature of things.

Opponents of such theories, following G. E. Moore, accuse them of committing "the naturalistic fallacy," since they identify an ethical judgment with a factual one. To call this a fallacy, however, without first showing that it is a mistake, as is sometimes done, is simply to beg the question. The critics also claim, therefore, that all proposed definitions of "good" and "right" in nonethical terms can be shown to be mistaken by a very simple argument, sometimes referred to as the "open question" argument. Suppose that a definist holds that "good" or "right" means "having the property P," for example, "being desired" or "being conducive to the greatest general happiness." Then, the argument is that we may agree that something has P, and yet ask significantly, "But is it good?" or "Is it right?" That is, we can sensibly say, "This has P, but is it good (or right)?" But if the proposed definition were correct, then we could not say this sensibly for it would be equivalent to saying, "This has P, but has it P?" which would be silly. Likewise, one can say, "This has P but it is not good (or right)," without contradicting oneself, which could not be the case if the definition were correct. Therefore the definition cannot be correct.

To this argument stated in such a simple form, as it almost always is, a definist may make several replies. (1) He may argue that the meaning of words like "good" and "right" in ordinary use is very unclear, so that when a clarifying definition of one of them is offered, it is almost certain not to retain all of what we vaguely associate with the term. Thus, the substitute cannot seem to be entirely the same as the original, and yet may turn out to be an acceptable definition. (2) He may point out that the term being defined may have a number of different uses, as we saw in the case of "good." Then P may be correct as an account of one of its uses, even though one can still say, "This has P, but is it good?" For one can agree, say, that X is good intrinsically, and still ask sensibly if it is good extrinsically, morally, or on the whole. (3) What we mean by some of our terms is often very hard to formulate, as Socrates and his interlocutors found. This means that one who doubts a certain formulation can always use the open question kind of an argument, but it does not mean that no definition can possibly be correct. (4) A definist like Perry may reply that the open question argument does show that the proposed definitions are not accurate accounts of what we mean by "good" and "right" in ordinary discourse, but that it still may be desirable to adopt them, all things considered. (5) A definist like Sharp, who thinks that his definitions do express what we actually mean, might even say that we cannot really ask significantly, "Is what we desire on reflection good?" or "Is what we approve when we take an impersonal point of view right?" His definitions are just plausible enough to give such a reply considerable force. In any case, however, although his critics may still be right, they will merely be begging the question if they rest their case on the open question argument.

The open question argument as usually stated, then, is insufficient to refute all definist theories. Its users almost never, in fact, make any serious effort to see what definists might say in reply or to consider their definitions seriously, as some of them certainly deserve to be. We cannot ourselves, however, try to consider separately all of the more plausible definitions which have been proposed. Even after studying them I find myself doubting that any pure definist theory, whether naturalistic or metaphysical, can be regarded as adequate as an account of what we do mean. For such a theory holds that an ethical judgment simply is an assertion of a fact—that ethical terms constitute merely an alternative vocabulary for reporting facts. It may be that they should be reinterpreted so that this is the case. In actual usage, however, this seems clearly not to be so. When we are making merely factual assertions we are not thereby taking any pro or con attitude toward what we are talking about; we are not recommending it, prescribing it, or anything of the sort. But when we make an ethical judgment we are not neutral in this way; it would seem paradoxical if one were to say "X is good" or "Y is right" but be absolutely indifferent to its being sought or done by himself or anyone else. If he were indifferent in this way, we would take him to mean that it is generally regarded as good or right, but that he did not so regard it himself. We may be making or implying factual assertions in some of our ethical judgments—when we say, "He was a good man," we do seem to imply that he was honest, kind, etc.—but this is not all that we are doing.

It might be replied, by Perry for example, that we ought to redefine our ethical terms so that they merely constitute another vocabulary for reporting certain empirical or metaphysical facts (perhaps on the ground that then our ethical judgments could be justified on the basis of science or metaphysics). Then we would have to consider whether we really need such an alternative way of reporting those facts, and whether we can get along without a special vocabulary to do what we have been using our ethical terms to do—which at least includes expressing pro or con attitudes, recommending, prescribing, evaluating, and so on.

It seems doubtful, then, that we can be satisfied with any pure definist theory of the meaning of moral and other value judgments. It also seems to me that such theories do not suffice to solve the problem of justification. If we accept a certain definition of "good," or "right," then, as we saw, we will know just how to justify judgments about what is good or right. But this means that the whole burden rests on the definition, and we may still ask how the definition is justified or why we should accept it. As far as I can see, when Perry tries to persuade us to accept his definition of "right," he is in effect persuading us to accept, as a basis for action, the ethical principle that what is conducive to harmonious happiness is right. He cannot establish his definition first and then show us that this principle is valid because it is true by definition. He cannot establish his definition unless he can convince us of the principle.

This may seem obvious, since Perry's definition is meant as a recommendation. But a definist who regards his definition as reportive, and not reforming, would presumably rejoin by saying that his definition is justified simply by the fact that it expresses what we ordinarily mean, just as dictionary definitions are justified. It has been claimed that the notion of obligation as we know it was not present in Greek times and is due to the Judeo-Christian theology. It might be held, then, that "ought," as it is actually used in our moral discourse, means "commanded by God," and many people would accept this as an account of what they mean. If we ask such a reportive theological definist why we ought to do what God commands, he will probably answer, if he understands us to be asking for a justification and not for motivation, that we ought to do this because "ought" simply means "commanded by God." But this, if true, would only show that his ethical principle had become enshrined in our moral discourse; it would not show why we should continue to give adherence to his principle, and this is the question. In other words, to advocate the adoption of or continued adherence to a definition of an ethical term seems to be tantamount to trying to justify the corresponding moral principle. Appealing to a definition in support of a principle is not a solution to the problem of justification, for the definition needs to be justified, and justifying it involves the same problems that justifying a principle does.

If this is true, then our basic ethical norms and values cannot be justified by grounding them in the nature of things in any strictly logical sense. For this can be done logically only if "right," "good," and "ought" can be defined in nonethical terms. Such definitions, however, turn out to be disguised ethical principles that cannot themselves be deduced logically from the nature of things. It follows that ethics does not depend *logically* on facts about man and the world, empirical or nonempirical, scientific or theological.

It still may be that there is some *non-logical* sense in which our basic norms and value judgments can be justified by appeal to the nature of things. We have already seen that ethical egoists seek to justify their theory of obligation by arguing that human nature is so constituted that each of us always pursues only his own good, and that Mill and other hedonists try to justify their theory of value by showing that human nature is so constituted as to desire nothing but pleasure or the means to pleasure. Neither the egoists nor the hedonists claim that their argument affords a strict logical proof. I have also indicated that such arguments nevertheless have a very considerable force, provided their premises are correct. But we saw reason to question the premises of the psychological arguments for egoism and hedonism, and hence must take them as inadequate. In any case, however, it is doubtful that one could find any similar "proofs" of principles like beneficence, justice, or utility.

Many people hold that morality depends on religion or theology—that ethical principles can be justified by appeal to theological premises and only by appeal to such premises. To those who hold this we must reply, in view of our argument, that this dependence cannot be a *logical* one. They may, of course, still maintain that morality is dependent on religion in some psychological way, for example, that no adequate motivation to be moral is possible without religion. This, I think, is true, if at all, only in a very qualified sense; however, even if religious beliefs and experiences are necessary for *motivation,* it does not follow that the *justification* of moral principles depends on such beliefs and experiences. Theologians may also contend that the law of love or beneficence can be rationally justified on theological grounds, even if it cannot rest on such grounds logically. They may argue, for instance, that if one fully believes or unquestionably experiences that God is love, then one must, if he is rational, conclude that he, too, should love. They may say that, although this conclusion does not follow logically, it would be unreasonable for one to draw any other or to refrain from drawing it. In this belief they may well be right; for all that I have said, I am inclined to think they are right. However, it does not follow that the principle of beneficence (let alone that of equality) *depends* on religion for its justification even in this non-logical sense. It may be that it can also be justified in some other way.

INTUITIONISM

We must, then, give up the notion that our basic principles and values can be justified by being shown to rest *logically* on true propositions about man and the world. We may also have to admit or insist that they cannot be justified satisfactorily by any such psychological arguments as are used by egoists and hedonists. But now another familiar answer to the question of justification presents itself—the view that our basic principles and value judgments are intuitive or self-evident and thus do not need to be justified by any kind of argument, logical or psychological, since they are self-justifying or, in Descartes's words, "clearly and distinctly true." This view was very strong until recently, and is held by many of the writers we have mentioned: Butler, Sidgwick, Rashdall, Moore, Prichard, Ross, Carritt, Hartmann, Ewing, and possibly even by Plato. It is sometimes called *intuitionism,* sometimes *non-naturalism.*

Intuitionism involves and depends on a certain theory about the meaning or nature of ethical judgments. Definist theories imply that ethical terms stand for properties of things, like being desired or being conducive to harmonious happiness, and that ethical judgments are simply statements ascribing these properties to things. Intuitionists agree to this, but deny that the properties referred to by words like "good" and "ought" are definable in nonethical terms. In fact, they insist that some of these properties are indefinable or simple and unanalyzable, as yellowness and pleasantness are. Sidgwick holds that "ought" stands for such a property, Moore that "good" does, and Ross that both do. These properties are not, therefore, unintelligible or unknown, anymore than pleasantness and yellowness are. But they are not natural or empirical properties as are pleasantness and yellowness. They are of a very different kind, being non-natural or nonempirical and, so to speak, normative rather than factual—different in kind from all the properties dreamed of in the philosophies of the definists. According to this view, as for the definists, ethical judgments are true or false; but they are not factual and cannot be justified by empirical observation or metaphysical reasoning. The basic ones, particular or general, are self-evident and can only be known by intuition; this follows, it is maintained, from the fact that the properties involved are simple and non-natural.

On this view, ethical judgments may be and are said to be rooted in the natures and relations of things, but not in the sense that they can be derived from propositions about man and the world, as the views previously discussed hold. They are based on the natures and relations of things in the sense that it is self-evident that a thing of a certain nature is good, for example, that what is pleasant or harmonious is good in itself; or that a being of a certain nature ought to treat another being of a certain nature in a certain way, for example, that one man ought to be just, kind, and truthful toward another man.

There are a number of reasons why intuitionism, for almost two centuries the standard view among moral philosophers, now finds few supporters. First of all, it raises several ontological and epistemological questions. An intuitionist must believe in simple indefinable properties, properties that are of a peculiar non-natural or normative sort, a priori or nonempirical concepts, intuition, and self-evident or synthetic necessary propositions. All of these beliefs are hard to defend. Do our ethical terms point to distinct and indefinable properties? It is not easy to be sure, and many philosophers cannot find such properties in their experience. It is also very difficult to understand what a non-natural property is like, and intuitionists have not been very satisfying on this point. Moreover, it is very difficult to defend the belief in a priori concepts and self-evident truths in ethics, now that mathematicians have generally given up the belief that there are such concepts and truths in their field.

Intuitionism is also not easy to square with prevailing theories in psychology and anthropology, even if we do not regard relativism as proved by them, a point we will take up later. An enriched view of the meanings of meaning and of the functions and uses of language likewise casts doubt on the view that ethical judgments are primarily property-ascribing assertions, as intuitionists, like definists, believe.

Intuitionism may still be true in spite of such considerations. But there are two arguments against it that many have regarded as decisive. Both are used by noncognitivists or nondescriptivists and, interestingly enough, the first is similar to the open question argument used against definists by intuitionists themselves. Let us suppose, it is said, that there are such brave non-natural and indefinable properties as the intuitionists talk about. Let us also suppose that act A has one of these properties, P. Then one can admit that A has P and still sensibly ask, "But why should I do A?" One could not do this if "I should do A" means "A has P"; hence it does not mean "A has P" as intuitionists think.

I do not find this argument convincing. "Why should I do A?" is an ambiguous question. One who asks it may be asking, "What motives are there for my doing A?" or he may be asking, "Am I really morally obligated to do A?" That is, he may be asking for *motivation* or he may be asking for *justification*. Now, of course, one can admit that A has P and still sensibly ask, "What motives are there for my doing that which has P?" But this, an intuitionist may say, is irrelevant, since he is proposing a theory of justification and not a theory of motivation, although he is also ready to provide a theory of motivation at the proper time. Therefore, the question is whether one can admit that A has P and still ask sensibly, "Ought I really to do A?" Here we must remember that the intuitionist holds that "I ought to do A" *means* "A has P" or, in other words, that P *is* the property of obligatoriness. Hence, he can answer the argument in its relevant form by saying that *if* "I ought to do A" does mean "A has P," then one cannot sensibly say, "A has P but ought I to do it?" His critic may still insist that he can sensibly say this, but not if he first admits that "I ought to do A" means "A has P." For him simply to assert that it does not mean "A has P" is to beg the question; however, his argument does not prove his conclusion, but assumes it. If there is a property of obligatoriness, as the intuitionist holds, then one cannot sensibly admit that A has this property and ask, "But is it obligatory?"

The second argument, which comes from Hume, is used against many kinds of definism as well as intuitionism, and has to do with motivation rather than justification. It begins with an insistence that ethical judgments are in themselves motivating or "practical" in the sense that, if one accepts such a judgment, he must have some motivation for acting according to it. It then contends that, if an ethical judgment merely ascribes a property, P, to something, then, whether P is natural or non-natural, one can accept the judgment and still have no motivation to act one way rather than another.

Intuitionists (and definists) also have a possible answer to this argument. They can maintain that we are so constituted that, if we recognize X to be right or good (i.e., that X has P), this will generate a pro attitude toward X in us, either by itself or by way of an innate desire for what has P. One may, of course, question their psychological claims, but one must at least give good reasons for thinking these are false before one takes this argument as final.

On the whole, however, intuitionism strikes me as implausible even if it has not been disproved. As was indicated earlier, ethical judgments do not seem to be mere property-ascribing statements, natural or non-natural; they express favorable or unfavorable attitudes (and do not merely generate them), recommend, prescribe, and the like. Of course, one could maintain that they do this and also ascribe simple non-natural properties to actions and things, but such a view still involves one in the difficulties mentioned a moment ago. The main point to be made now is that the belief in self-evident ethical truths, and all that goes with it, is so difficult to defend that it seems best to look for some other answer to the problem of justification.

NONCOGNITIVE OR NONDESCRIPTIVIST THEORIES

The third general type of theory of the meaning or nature of ethical judgments has no very satisfactory label. However, it has been called noncognitivist or nondescriptivist because, as against both definists and intuitionists, it holds that ethical judgments are not assertions or statements ascribing properties to (or denying them of) actions, persons, or things, and insists that they have a very different "logic," meaning, or use. It embraces a wide variety of views, some more and others much less extreme.

1. The most extreme of these are a number of views that deny ethical judgments, or at least the most basic ones, to be capable of any kind of rational or objectively valid justification. On one such view—that of A. J. Ayer—they are simply expressions of emotion much like ejaculations. Saying that killing is wrong is like saying, "Killing, boo!" It says nothing true or false and cannot be justified in any rational way. Rudolf Carnap once took a similar view, except that he interpreted "Killing is wrong" as a command, "Do not kill," rather than as an ejaculation. Bertrand Russell held that moral judgments merely express a certain kind of wish. Many existentialists likewise regard basic ethical judgments, particular or general, as arbitrary commitments or decisions for which no justification can be given.

I should point out here that such irrationalistic views about ethical judgments are not held only by atheistic positivists and existentialists. They are also held by at least some religious existentialists and by other theologians. For example, a theologian who maintains that the basic principles of ethics are divine commands is taking a position much like Carnap's. If he adds that God's commands are arbitrary and cannot be justified rationally, then his position is no less extreme. If he holds that God's commands are, at least in principle, rationally defensible, then his position is like the less extreme ones to be described.

2. C. L. Stevenson's form of the emotive theory is somewhat less extreme than Ayer's. He argues that ethical judgments express the speaker's attitudes and evoke, or seek to evoke, similar attitudes in the hearer. But he realizes that to a very considerable extent our attitudes are based on our beliefs, and so can be reasoned about. For example, I may favor a certain course of action because I believe it has or will have certain results. I will then advance the fact that it has these results as an argument in its favor. But you may argue that it does not have these results, and if you can show this, my attitude may change and I may withdraw my judgment that the course of action in question is right or good. In a sense, you have refuted me. But, of course, this is only because of an underlying attitude on my part of being in favor of certain results rather than others. Stevenson goes on to suggest that our most basic attitudes, and the ethical judgments in which we express them, may not be rooted in beliefs of any kind, in which case they cannot be reasoned about in any way. He is open-minded about this, however, and allows a good deal of room for a kind of argument and reasoning.

3. More recently, from a number of Oxford philosophers and others, we have had still less extreme views. They refuse to regard ethical judgments as mere expressions or evocations of feeling or attitude, as mere commands, or as arbitrary decisions or commitments. Rather, they regard them as evaluations, recommendations, prescriptions, and the like; and they stress the fact that such judgments imply that we are willing to generalize or universalize them and are ready to reason about them, points with which we have agreed. That is, they point out that when we say of something that it is good or right, we imply that there are reasons for our judgment which are not purely persuasive and private in their cogency. They are even ready to say that such a judgment may be called true or false, though it is very different from "X is yellow" or "Y is to the left of Z." For them ethical judgments are essentially reasoned acts of evaluating, recommending, and prescribing.

The arguments for such theories—the open question argument against definists and the two arguments against intuitionists—we have found to be less conclusive than they are thought to be. To my mind, nevertheless, these theories, or rather the least extreme of them, are on the right track. The kind of account the latter give of the meaning and nature of ethical judgments is acceptable as far as it goes. Such judgments do not simply say that something has or does not have a certain property. Neither are they mere expressions of emotion, will, or decision. They do more than just express or indicate the speaker's attitudes. They evaluate, instruct, recommend, prescribe, advise, and so on; and they claim or imply that what they do is rationally justified or justifiable, which mere expressions of emotion and commands do not do. The more extreme views, therefore, are mistaken as a description of the nature of ethical judgments. Moreover, it is not necessary to agree with them that such judgments cannot be justified in any important sense. They generally assume that if such judgments are not self-evident and cannot be proved inductively or deductively on the basis of empirical or nonempirical facts, as we have seen to be the case, then it follows that they are purely arbitrary. But this does not follow. It may be that this conception of rational justification is too narrow, as I have already intimated in discussing psychological egoism and hedonism. Mill may be right when he says, near the end of Chapter I of *Utilitarianism,*

> We are not...to infer that [the acceptance or rejection of an ethical first principle] must depend on blind impulse, or arbitrary choice. There is a larger meaning of the word "proof," in which this question is...amenable to it...The subject is within the cognizance of the rational faculty; and neither does that faculty deal with it solely in the way of intuition. Considerations may be presented capable of determining the intellect either to give or withhold its assent...

Here, Mill is with the less extreme of the recent nondescriptive theories, as against the definists, the intuitionists, and the more extreme nondescriptivists. All of these share the conception of justification as consisting either in self-evidence or in inductive or deductive proof. Only the definists and intuitionists believe that ethical judgments can be justified in one or the other of these ways, while positivists and existentialists deny that ethical judgments can be justified at all. Mill and the less extreme recent philosophers, on the other hand, agree with intuitionists and definists that they can be justified in some rational sense or in some "larger meaning of the word 'proof'," though they have different and various views about the nature of such justification.

At this point, it may help to notice that even such things as "mere" expressions of feeling and commands may be justified or unjustified, rational or irrational. Suppose that A is angry at B, believing B to have insulted him. C may be able to show A that his anger is unjustified, since B has not actually insulted him at all. If A simply goes on being angry, although he no longer has any reason, we should regard his anger as quite irrational. Again, if an officer commands a private to close the door, believing it to be open when it is not, it is reasonable for the private to answer, "But, sir, the door is closed," and it would be quite irrational if the officer were seriously to command the private to close it anyway. Emotions and commands, generally at least, have a background of beliefs and are justified or unjustified, rational or irrational, depending on whether these beliefs themselves are so.

APPROACH TO AN ADEQUATE THEORY

In my opinion, even the less extreme of recent nondescriptivist theories have not gone far enough. They have been too ready to admit a kind of basic relativism after all. They insist that ethical judgments imply the presence of, or at least the possibility of giving, reasons which justify them. But they almost invariably allow or even insist that the validity of these reasons is ultimately relative, either to the individual or to his culture, and, therefore, conflicting basic judgments may both be justified or justifiable. Now, it may be that in the end one must agree with this view, but most recent discussions entirely neglect a fact about ethical judgments on which Ewing has long insisted, namely, that they make or somehow imply a claim to be objectively and rationally justified or valid. In other words, an ethical judgment claims that it will stand up under scrutiny by oneself and others in the light of the most careful thinking and the best knowledge, and that rival judgments will not stand up under such scrutiny. Hume makes the point nicely, though only for *moral* judgments:

> The notion of morals implies some sentiment common to all mankind, which recommends the same object to general approbation.... When a man denominates another his *enemy,* his *rival,* his *antagonist,* his *adversary,* he is understood to speak the language of self-love, and to express sentiments, peculiar to himself, and arising from his particular circumstance and situation. But when he bestows on any man the epithets of *vicious* or *odious* or *depraved,* he then speaks another language, and expresses sentiments, in which he expects all his audience are to concur with him. He must here...depart from his private and particular situation, and must choose a point of view, common to himself with others....[4]

And, he must claim, Hume might have added, that anyone else who takes this point of view and from it reviews the relevant facts will come to the same conclusion. In fact, he goes on to suggest that precisely because we need or want a language in which to express, not just sentiments peculiar to ourselves but sentiments in which we expect all men are to concur with us, another language in which we may claim that our sentiments are justified and valid, we had to

> ...invent a peculiar set of terms, in order to express those universal sentiments of censure or approbation.... Virtue and vice become then known; morals are recognized; certain general ideas are framed of human conduct and behavior....

This kind of an account of our normative discourse strikes me as eminently wise. It is a language in which we may express our sentiments—approvals, disapprovals, evaluations, recommendations, advice, instructions, prescriptions—and put them out into the public arena for rational scrutiny and discussion, claiming that they will hold up under such scrutiny and discussion and that all our audience will concur with us if they will also choose the same common point of view. That this is so is indicated by the fact that if A makes an ethical judgment about X and then, upon being challenged by B, says, "Well, at least I'm in favor of X," we think he has backed down. He has shifted from the language of public dialogue to that of mere self-revelation. This view recognizes the claim to objective validity on which intuitionists and definists alike insist, but it also recognizes the force of much recent criticism of such views.

[4] *An Enquiry into the Principles of Morals,* pp. 113–14.

RELATIVISM Against any such view it will be argued, of course, that this claim to be objectively and rationally justified or valid, in the sense of holding up against all rivals through an impartial and informed examination, is simply mistaken and must be given up. This is the contention of the relativist and we must consider it now, although we can do so only briefly.

Actually, we must distinguish at least three forms of relativism. First, there is what may be called *descriptive relativism.* When careful, it does not say merely that the ethical judgments of different people and societies are different. For this would be true even if people and societies agreed in their basic ethical judgments and differed only in their *derivative* ones. What careful descriptive relativism says is that the *basic* ethical beliefs of different people and societies are different and even conflicting. I stress this because the fact that in some primitive societies children believe they should put their parents to death before they get old, whereas we do not, does not prove descriptive relativism. These primitive peoples may believe this because they think their parents will be better off in the hereafter if they enter it while still able-bodied; if this is the case, their ethics and ours are alike in that they rest on the precept that children should do the best they can for their parents. The divergence, then, would be in factual, rather than in ethical, beliefs.

Second, there is *meta-ethical relativism,* which is the view we must consider. It holds that, in the case of basic ethical judgments, there is no objectively valid, rational way of justifying one against another; consequently, two conflicting basic judgments may be equally valid.

The third form of relativism is *normative relativism.* While descriptive relativism makes an anthropological or sociological assertion and meta-ethical relativism a meta-ethical one, this form of relativism puts forward a normative principle: what is right or good for one individual or society is not right or good for another, even if the situations involved are similar, meaning not merely that what is thought right or good by one is not thought right or good by another (this is just descriptive relativism over again), but that what is really right or good in the one case is not so in another. Such a normative principle seems to violate the requirements of consistency and universalization mentioned earlier. We need not consider it here, except to point out that it cannot be justified by appeal to either of the other forms of relativism and does not follow from them. One can be a relativist of either of the other sorts without believing that the same kind of conduct is right for one person or group and wrong for another. One can, for example, believe that everyone ought to treat people equally, though recognizing that not everyone admits this and holding that one's belief cannot be justified.

Our question is about the second kind of relativism. The usual argument used to establish it rests on descriptive relativism. Now, descriptive relativism has not been incontrovertibly established. Some cultural anthropologists and social psychologists have even questioned its truth, for example, Ralph Linton and S. E. Asch. However, to prove meta-ethical relativism one must prove more than descriptive relativism. One must also prove that people's basic ethical judgments would differ and conflict even if they were fully enlightened and shared all the same factual beliefs. It is not enough to show that people's basic ethical judgments are different, for such differences might all be due to differences and incompletenesses in their factual beliefs, as in the example of the primitive societies used previously. In this case, it would still be possible to hold that some basic ethical judgments can be justified as valid to everyone, in principle at least, if not in practice.

It is, however, extremely difficult to show that people's basic ethical judgments would still be different even if they were fully enlightened, conceptually clear, shared the same factual beliefs, and were taking the same point of view. To show this, one would have to find clear cases in which all of these conditions are fulfilled and people still differ. Cultural anthropologists do not show us such cases; in all of their cases, there are differences in conceptual understanding and factual belief. Even when one takes two people in the same culture, one cannot be sure that all of the necessary conditions are fulfilled. I conclude, therefore, that meta-ethical relativism has not been proved and, hence, that we need not, in our ethical judgments, give up the claim that they are objectively valid in the sense that they will be sustained by a review by all those who are free, clear-headed, fully informed, and who take the point of view in question.

A THEORY OF JUSTIFICATION

We now have the beginnings of a theory of the meaning and justification of ethical judgments. To go any farther, we must distinguish moral judgments proper from nonmoral normative judgments and say something separately about the justification of each. How can we distinguish moral from other normative judgments? Not by the words used in them, for words like "good" and "right" all have nonmoral as well as moral uses. By the feelings that accompany them? The difficulty in this proposal is that it is hard to tell which feelings are moral except by seeing what judgments they go with. It is often thought that moral judgments are simply whatever judgments we regard as overriding all other normative judgments in case of conflict, but then aesthetic or prudential judgments become moral ones if we take them to have priority over others, which seems paradoxical. It seems to me that what makes some normative judgments moral, some aesthetic, and some prudential is the fact that different points of view are taken in the three cases, and that the point of view taken is indicated by the kinds of reasons that are given. Consider three judgments: (a) I say that you ought to do X and give as the reason the fact that X will help you succeed in business; (b) I say you should do Y and cite as the reason the fact that Y will produce a striking contrast of colors; and (c) I say you should do Z and give as the reason the fact that Z will keep a promise or help someone. Here the reason I give reveals the point of view I am taking and the kind of judgment I am making.

Now let us take up the justification of nonmoral normative judgments. We are interested primarily in judgments of intrinsic value such as were discussed in the previous chapter, for such judgments are relevant to ethics because, through the principle of beneficence, the question of what is good or bad comes to bear on the question of what is right or wrong. Besides, if we know how to justify judgments of intrinsic value, we will know how to justify judgments of extrinsic and inherent value, for judgments of the latter sorts presuppose judgments of the former. It is true, as we have already seen, that we cannot *prove* basic judgments of intrinsic value in any strict sense of proof, but this fact does not mean that we cannot justify them or reasonably claim them to be justified. But how can we do this? By taking what I shall call the evaluative point of view as such, unqualified by any such adjective as "aesthetic," "moral," or "prudential," and then trying to see what judgment we are led to make when we do so, considering the thing in question wholly on the basis of its intrinsic character, not its consequences or conditions. What is it to take the nonmorally evaluative point of view? It is to be free, informed, clear-headed, impartial, willing to universalize; in general, it is to be "calm" and "cool," as Butler would say, in one's consideration of such items as pleasure, knowledge, and love, for the question is simply what it is rational to choose. This is what we tried to do in Chapter 5. If one considers an item in this reflective way and comes out in favor of it, one is rationally justified in judging it to be intrinsically good, even if one cannot prove one's judgment. In doing so, one claims that everyone else who does likewise will concur; and one's judgment is really justified if this claim is correct, which, of course, one can never know for certain. If others who also claim to be calm and cool do not concur, one must reconsider to see if both sides are really taking the evaluative point of view, considering only intrinsic features, clearly understanding one another, and so on. More one cannot do and, if disagreement persists, one may still claim to be right (i.e., that others will concur eventually if . . .); but one must be open-minded and tolerant. In fact, we saw in Chapter 5 that one may have to admit a certain relativity in the ranking of things listed as intrinsically good, although possibly not in the listing itself.

What about the justification of moral judgments? Already in Chapters 2 and 3 we have, in effect, said something about the justification of judgments of right, wrong, and obligation. We argued that a particular judgment essentially entails a general one, so that one cannot regard a particular judgment as justified unless one is also willing to accept the entailed general one, and vice versa. This is true whether we are speaking of judgments of actual or of prima facie duty. We have also seen that judgments of actual duty, whether particular judgments or rules, cannot simply be deduced from the basic principles of beneficence and justice, even with the help of factual premises, since these must be taken as prima facie principles and may conflict on occasion. Thus, we have two questions: first, how can we justify judgments of actual duty, general or particular, and second, how can we justify basic principles of prima facie duty? The same answer, however, will do for both. It seems fair to assume that it will also do for the question of justifying judgments of moral value.

First, we must take the moral point of view, as Hume indicated, not that of self-love or aesthetic judgment, nor the more general point of view involved in judgments of intrinsic value. We must also be free, impartial, willing to universalize, conceptually clear, and informed about all possibly relevant facts. Then we are justified in judging that a certain act or kind of action is right, wrong, or obligatory, and in claiming that our judgment is objectively valid, at least as long as no one who is doing likewise disagrees. Our judgment or principle is really justified if it holds up under sustained scrutiny of this sort from the moral point of view on the part of everyone. Suppose we encounter someone who claims to be doing this but comes to a different conclusion. Then we must do our best, through reconsideration and discussion, to see if one of us is failing to meet the conditions in some way. If we can detect no failing on either side and still disagree, we may and I think still must each claim to be correct, for the conditions never are perfectly fulfilled by both of us and one of us may turn out to be mistaken after all. If what was said about relativism is true, we cannot both be correct. But both of us must be open-minded and tolerant if we are to go on living within the moral institution of life and not resort to force or other immoral or nonmoral devices.

If this line of thought is acceptable, then we may say that a basic moral judgment, principle, or code is justified or "true" if it is or will be agreed to by everyone who takes the moral point of view and is clearheaded and logical and knows all that is relevant about himself, mankind, and the universe. Are our own principles of beneficence and justice justified or "true" in this sense? The argument in Chapters 2 and 3 was essentially an attempt to take the moral point of view and from it to review various normative theories and arrive at one of our own. Our principles have not been proved, but perhaps it may be claimed that they will be concurred in by those who try to do likewise. This claim was implicitly made in presenting them. Whether the claim is true or not must wait upon the scrutiny of others.

The fact that moral judgments claim a consensus on the part of others does not mean that the individual thinker must bow to the judgment of the majority in his society. He is not claiming an *actual* consensus, he is claiming that in the end—which never comes or comes only on the Day of Judgment —his position will be concurred in by those who freely and clear-headedly review the relevant facts from the moral point of view. In other words, he is claiming an *ideal* consensus that transcends majorities and actual societies. One's society and its code and institutions may be wrong. Here enters the autonomy of the moral agent—he must take the moral point of view and must claim an eventual consensus with others who do so, but he must judge for himself. He may be mistaken, but, like Luther, he cannot do otherwise. Similar remarks hold for one who makes nonmoral judgments.

THE MORAL POINT OF VIEW

What is the moral point of view? This is a crucial question for the view we have suggested. It is also one on which there has been much controversy lately. According to one theory, one is taking the moral point of view if and only if one is willing to universalize one's maxims. Kant would probably accept this if he were alive. But I pointed out that one may be willing to universalize from a prudential point of view; and also that what one is willing to universalize is not necessarily a moral rule. Other such formal characterizations of the moral point of view have been proposed. A more plausible characterization to my mind, however, is that of Kurt Baier. He holds that one is taking the moral point of view if one is not being egoistic, one is doing things on principle, one is willing to universalize one's principles, and in doing so one considers the good of everyone alike.[5]

Hume thought that the moral point of view was that of sympathy, and it seems to me he was on the right wavelength. I have already argued that the point of view involved in a judgment can be identified by the kind of reason that is given for the judgment when it is made or if it is challenged. Then the moral point of view can be identified by determining what sorts of facts are reasons for moral judgments or moral reasons. Roughly following Hume, I now want to suggest that moral reasons consist of facts about what actions, dispositions, and persons do to the lives of sentient beings, including beings other than the agent in question, and that the moral point of view is that which is concerned about such facts. My own position, then, is that one is taking the moral point of view if and only if (a) one is making normative judgments about actions, desires, dispositions, intentions, motives, persons, or traits of character; (b) one is willing to universalize one's judgments; (c) one's reasons for one's judgments consist of facts about what the things judged do to the lives of sentient beings in terms of promoting or distributing nonmoral good and evil; and (d) when the judgment is about oneself or one's own actions, one's reasons include such facts about what one's own actions and dispositions do to the lives of other sentient beings as such, if others are affected. One has a morality or moral action-guide only if and

[5] *The Moral Point of View* (New York: Random House, 1965), Chap. 5.

insofar as one makes normative judgments from this point of view and is guided by them.

WHY BE MORAL? Another problem that remains has been mentioned before. Why should we be moral? Why should we take part in the moral institution of life? Why should we adopt the moral point of view? We have already seen that the question, "Why should . . . ?" is ambiguous, and may be a request either for motivation or for justification. Here, then, one may be asking for (1) the motives for doing what is morally right, (2) a justification for doing what is morally right, (3) motivation for adopting the moral point of view and otherwise subscribing to the moral institution of life, or (4) a justification of morality and the moral point of view. It is easy to see the form an answer to a request for (1) and (3) must take; it will consist in pointing out the various prudential and non-prudential motives for doing what is right or for participating in the moral institution of life. Most of these are familiar or readily thought of and need not be detailed here. A request for (2) might be taken as a request for a *moral* justification for doing what is right. Then, the answer is that doing what is morally right does not need a justification, since the justification has already been given in showing that it is right. On this interpretation, a request for (2) is like asking, "Why morally ought I to do what is morally right?" A request for (2) may also, however, be meant as a demand for a nonmoral justification of doing what is morally right; then, the answer to it will be like the answer to a request for (4). For a request for (4), being a request for reasons for subscribing to the moral way of thinking, judging, and living, must be a request for a nonmoral justification of morality. What will this be like?

There seem to be two questions here. First, why should *society* adopt such an institution as morality? Why should it foster such a system for the guidance of conduct in addition to convention, law, and prudence? To this the answer seems clear. The conditions of a satisfactory human life for people living in groups could hardly obtain otherwise. The alternatives would seem to be either a state of nature in which all or most of us would be worse off than we are, even if Hobbes is wrong in thinking that life in such a state would be "solitary, poor, nasty, brutish, and short"; or a leviathan civil state more totalitarian than any yet dreamed of, one in which the laws would cover all aspects of life and every possible deviation by the individual would be closed off by an effective threat of force.

The other question has to do with the nonmoral reasons (not just motives) there are for an *individual's* adopting the moral way of thinking and living. To some extent, the answer has just been given, but only to some extent. For on reading the last paragraph an individual might say, "Yes. This shows that society requires morality and even that it is to my advantage to have others adopt the moral way of life. But it does not show that I should adopt it, and certainly not that I should *always* act according to it. And it is no use arguing on moral grounds that I should. I want a nonmoral justification for thinking I should." Now, if this means that he wants to be shown that it is always to his advantage—that is, that his life will invariably be better or, at least, not worse in the prudential sense of better and worse—if he thoroughly adopts the moral way of life, then I doubt that his demand can always be met. Through the use of various familiar arguments, one can show that the moral way of life is likely to be to his advantage, but it must be admitted in all honesty that one who takes the moral road may be called upon to make a sacrifice and, hence, may not have as good a life in the nonmoral sense as he would otherwise have had.

The point made at the end of Chapter 5 must be recalled here, namely, that morally good or right action is one kind of excellent activity and hence is a prime candidate for election as part of any good life, especially since it is a kind of excellent activity of which all normal people are capable. It does seem to me that this is an important consideration in the answer to our present question. Even if we add it to the usual arguments, however, we still do not have a conclusive proof that every individual should, in the nonmoral sense under discussion, always do the morally excellent thing. For, as far as I can see, from a prudential point of view, some individuals might have nonmorally better lives if they sometimes did what is not morally excellent, for example in cases in which a considerable self-sacrifice is morally required. A TV speaker once said of his subject, "He was too good for his good," and it seems to me that this may sometimes be true.

It does not follow that one cannot justify the ways of morality to an individual, although it may follow that one cannot justify morality to some individuals. For nonmoral justification is not necessarily egoistic or prudential. If A asks B why he, A, should be moral, B may reply by asking A to try to decide in a rational way what kind of a life he wishes to live or what kind of a person he wishes to be. That is, B may ask A what way of life A would choose if he were to choose rationally, or in other words, freely, impartially, and in full knowledge of what it is like to live the various alternative ways of life, including the moral one. B may then be able to convince A, when he is calm and cool in this way, that the way of life he prefers, all things considered, includes the moral way of life. If so, then he has justified the moral way of life to A. A may even, when he considers matters in such a way, prefer a life that includes self-sacrifice on his part.

Of course, A may refuse to be rational, calm, and cool. He may retort, "But why should I be rational?" However, if this was his posture in originally asking for justification, he had no business asking for it. For one can only ask for justification if one is willing to be rational. One cannot consistently ask for reasons unless one is ready to accept reasons of some sort. Even in asking, "Why should I be rational?" one is implicitly committing oneself to rationality, for such a commitment is part of the connotation of the word "should."

What kind of a life A would choose if he were fully rational and knew all about himself and the world will, of course, depend on what sort of a person he is (and people are different), but if psychological egoism is not true of any of us, it may always be that A would then choose a way of life that would be moral. As Bertrand Russell once wrote:

> We have wishes which are not purely personal. . . The sort of life that most of us admire is one which is guided by large, impersonal desires. . . Our desires are, in fact, more general and less purely selfish than many moralists imagine. . .[6]

Perhaps A has yet one more question: Is society justified in demanding that I adopt the moral way of life, and in blaming and censuring me if I do not?" But this is a moral question; and A can hardly expect it to be allowed that society is justified in doing this to A only if it can show that doing so is to A's advantage. However, if A is asking whether society is morally justified in requiring of him at least a certain minimal subscription to the moral institution of life, then the answer surely is that society sometimes is justified in this, as Socrates argued in the *Crito*. But society must be careful here. For it is itself morally required to respect the individual's autonomy and liberty, and in general to treat him justly; and it must remember that morality is made to minister to the good lives of individuals and not to interfere with them any more than is necessary. Morality is made for man, not man for morality.

6 *Religion and Science* (New York: Henry Holt and Co., 1935), pp. 252–54.

FOR FURTHER READING

Introductory Readings in Ethics, edited by William K. Frankena and John T. Granrose, contains readings that are very closely correlated, chapter by chapter, with the discussions in this book and may be consulted in connection with most of the authors, topics, or questions covered.

The following bibliography is not intended to be complete. More complete bibliographies can be found in the volume just referred to, or in the works of Hospers, Brandt, or Garner and Rosen listed below.

In connection with each of my chapters, readers will find helpful corresponding discussions in the introductory textbooks listed below, for example, in those of Hospers or Garner and Rosen.

INTRODUCTORY ANTHOLOGIES

Brandt, R. B., ed., *Value and Obligation.* New York: Harcourt Brace Jovanovich, Inc., 1961.

Frankena, W. K., and J. T. Granrose, eds., *Introductory Readings in Ethics.* Englewood Cliffs, N.J.: Prentice-Hall, Inc., 1974.

Jones, W. T., Frederick Sontag, M. O. Beckner, and R. J. Fogelin, eds., *Approaches to Ethics,* second edition. New York: McGraw-Hill, Inc., 1969. Selections from Plato to the present, chronologically arranged.

Melden, A. I., ed., *Ethical Theories,* second edition, with revisions. Englewood Cliffs, N.J.: Prentice-Hall, Inc., 1967. Selections from Plato to the early twentieth century, chronologically arranged.

Taylor, P. W., ed., *Problems of Moral Philosophy,* second edition. Belmont, Calif.: Dickenson Publishing Company, Inc., 1972.

ANTHOLOGIES OF CONTEMPORARY MORAL PHILOSOPHY

Margolis, Joseph, ed., *Contemporary Ethical Theory.* New York: Random House, 1966.

Pahel, Kenneth, and Marvin Schiller, eds., *Readings in Contemporary Ethical Theory.* Englewood Cliffs, N.J.: Prentice-Hall, Inc., 1970.

Sellars, W. S., and John Hospers, eds., *Readings in Ethical Theory,* second edition. New York: Appleton-Century-Crofts, Inc., 1970.

Thomson, J. J., and Gerald Dworkin, eds., *Ethics.* New York: Harper & Row, 1968.

SHORT INTRODUCTIONS TO ETHICS

Atkinson, R. F., *Conduct: An Introduction to Moral Philosophy.* London: Macmillan, 1969.

Dewey, John, *Theory of the Moral Life,* ed. Arnold Isenberg. New York: Holt, Rinehart and Winston, Inc., 1960. An important book in its own right.

Ewing, A. C., *Ethics.* New York: The Free Press, 1965.

Mabbott, J. D., *An Introduction to Ethics.* London: Hutchinson & Co., Ltd., 1966.

Moore, G. E., *Ethics.* New York: Oxford University Press, 1965. Unusually careful and hence a bit difficult.

Nielsen, Kai, "Problems of Ethics" in *The Encyclopedia of Philosophy,* ed. Paul Edwards. New York: The Macmillan Company and The Free Press, 1967. Volume Three, pages 117–34.

LONGER INTRODUCTIONS TO ETHICS

Brandt, R. B., *Ethical Theory.* Englewood Cliffs, N.J.: Prentice-Hall, Inc., 1959. Somewhat advanced for a beginner.

Garner, R. T., and Bernard Rosen, *Moral Philosophy.* New York: The Macmillan Company, 1967.

Gert, Bernard, *The Moral Rules.* New York: Harper & Row, 1970.

Hospers, John, *Human Conduct,* shorter edition. Harcourt Brace Jovanovich, Inc., 1972.

HISTORIES OF ETHICS

Abelson, Raziel, and Kai Nielsen, "History of Ethics" in *The Encyclopedia of Philosophy,* ed. Paul Edwards. New York: The Macmillan Company and The Free Press, 1967. Volume Three, pages 81–117.

Bourke, V. J., *History of Ethics,* in two volumes. New York: Doubleday & Company, 1970.

Hudson, W. D., *Modern Moral Philosophy.* New York: Doubleday & Company, Inc., 1970.

MacIntyre, Alasdair, A *Short History of Ethics.* New York: The Macmillan Company, 1966.

McGreal, I. P., *Problems of Ethics.* Scranton, Pa.: Chandler Publishing Company, 1970. Elementary.

Sidgwick, Henry, *Outlines of the History of Ethics.* New York: St Martin's Press, Inc., 1967. Good but a bit difficult.

WARNOCK, G. J., *Contemporary Moral Philosophy.* New York: St Martin's Press, Inc., 1967. Part of a series, "New Studies in Ethics," which includes helpful books on Kantian, Hegelian, Marxist, and existentialist ethics, among others.

READINGS ON MORAL PROBLEMS

ATKINSON, RONALD, *Sexual Morality.* London: Hutchinson & Co., Ltd., 1965.

BECK, R. N., and J. B. ORR, eds., *Ethical Choice.* New York: The Free Press, 1970.

BEDAU, H. A., ed., *Justice and Equality.* Englewood Cliffs, N.J.: Prentice-Hall, Inc., 1971.

GIRVETZ, H. K., ed., *Contemporary Moral Issues,* second edition. Belmont, Calif.: Wadsworth Publishing Company, Inc., 1968.

MELDEN, A. I., ed., *Human Rights.* Belmont, Calif.: Wadsworth Publishing Company, Inc., 1970.

MURPHY, J. G., ed., *Civil Disobedience and Violence.* Belmont, Calif.: Wadsworth Publishing Company, Inc., 1971.

RACHELS, JAMES, ed., *Moral Problems.* New York: Harper & Row, 1971.

WASSERSTROM, R. A., ed., *War and Morality.* Belmont, Calif.: Wadsworth Publishing Company, Inc., 1970.

WILSON, JOHN, NORMAN WILLIAMS, and BARRY SUGARMAN, *Introduction to Moral Education.* Baltimore: Penguin Books, Inc., 1967

WILSON, JOHN, *Logic and Sexual Morality.* Baltimore: Penguin Books, Inc., 1965.

INDEX